Software Testing and Tooling Courseware

-

Based on CTAP

Colophon

Title: Software Testing and Tooling Courseware - Based on CTAP

Authors: Rob Flier

Publisher: Van Haren Publishing, ‘s-Hertogenbosch

ISBN Hard Copy: 978 94 018 1282 5

Edition: First edition, first print, February 2025

Design: Van Haren Publishing, ‘s-Hertogenbosch

For further information about Van Haren Publishing please e-mail us at: info@vanharen.net
or visit our website: www.vanharen.net

Publisher about the Courseware

The Courseware was created by experts from the industry who served as the author(s) for this publication. The input for the material is based on existing publications and the experience and expertise of the author(s). The material has been revised by trainers who also have experience working with the material. Close attention was also paid to the key learning points to ensure what needs to be mastered.

The objective of the courseware is to provide maximum support to the trainer and to the student, during his or her training. The material has a modular structure and according to the author(s) has the highest success rate should the student opt for examination. The Courseware is also accredited for this reason, wherever applicable.

In order to satisfy the requirements for accreditation the material must meet certain quality standards. The structure, the use of certain terms, diagrams and references are all part of this accreditation. Additionally, the material must be made available to each student in order to obtain full accreditation. To optimally support the trainer and the participant of the training assignments, practice exams and results are provided with the material.

Direct reference to advised literature is also regularly covered in the sheets so that students can find additional information concerning a particular topic. The decision to leave out notes pages from the Courseware was to encourage students to take notes throughout the material.

Although the courseware is complete, the possibility that the trainer deviates from the structure of the sheets or chooses to not refer to all the sheets or commands does exist. The student always has the possibility to cover these topics and go through them on their own time. It is recommended to follow the structure of the courseware and publications for maximum exam preparation.

The courseware and the recommended literature are the perfect combination to learn and understand the theory.

-- Van Haren Publishing

Other publications by Van Haren Publishing

Van Haren Publishing (VHP) specializes in titles on Best Practices, methods and standards within four domains:

- IT and IT Management
- Architecture (Enterprise and IT)
- Business Management and
- Project Management

Van Haren Publishing is also publishing on behalf of leading organizations and companies: ASLBiSL Foundation, BRMI, CA, Centre Henri Tudor, Gaming Works, IACCM, IAOP, IFDC, Innovation Value Institute, IPMA-NL, ITSqc, NAF, KNVI, PMI-NL, PON, The Open Group, The SOX Institute.

Topics are (per domain):

IT and IT Management
ABC of ICT
ASL®
CATS CM®
CMMI®
COBIT®
e-CF
ISO/IEC 20000
ISO/IEC 27001/27002
ISPL
IT4IT®
IT-CMF™
IT Service CMM
ITIL®
MOF
MSF
SABSA
SAF
SIAM™
TRIM
VeriSM™

Enterprise Architecture
ArchiMate®
GEA®
Novius Architectuur Methode
TOGAF®

Business Management
BABOK® Guide
BiSL® and BiSL® Next
BRMBOK™
BTF
EFQM
eSCM
IACCM
ISA-95
ISO 9000/9001
OPBOK
SixSigma
SOX
SqEME®

Project Management
A4-Projectmanagement
DSDM/Atern
ICB / NCB
ISO 21500
MINCE®
M_o_R®
MSP®
P3O®
PMBOK® Guide
Praxis®
PRINCE2®

For the latest information on VHP publications, visit our website: www.vanharen.net.

Table of content

Self-Reflection of understanding Diagram

'What you do not measure, you cannot control.'' – Tom Peters

Fill in this diagram to self-evaluate your understanding of the material. This is an evaluation of how well you know the material and how well you understand it. In order to pass the exam successfully you should be aiming to reach the higher end of Level 3. If you really want to become a pro, then you should be aiming for Level 4. Your overall level of understanding will naturally follow the learning curve. So, it's important to keep track of where you are at each point of the training and address any areas of difficulty.

Based on where you are within the Self-Reflection of Understanding diagram you can evaluate the progress of your own training.

Level of Understanding	*Before Training (Pre-knowledge)*	*Training Part 1 (1st Half)*	*Training Part 2 (2nd Half)*	*After studying / reading the book*	*After exercises and the Practice exam*
Level 4 *I can explain the content and apply it .*					
Level 3 *I get it!* *I am right where I am supposed to be.*					Ready for the exam!
Level 2 *I almost have it but could use more practice.*					
Level 1 *I am learning but don't quite get it yet.*					

(Self-Reflection of Understanding Diagram)

Write down the problem areas that you are still having difficulty with so that you can consolidate them yourself, or with your trainer. After you have had a look at these, then you should evaluate to see if you now have a better understanding of where you actually are on the learning curve.

Troubleshooting

Problem areas: *Topic:*

Part 1

Part 2

You have gone through the book and studied.

You have answered the questions and done the practice exam.

Agenda

Day 1

Testtool overview

- What is test automation (a goal in itself)?

Working with tools for the

- Graphical User Interface
- Programming Interface

Testtool selection

- Tool adoption
- Tool selection

Working with:

- Graphical User Interface
- Robot Framework

Day 2

Test roles

Continuous testing

Working with

- Robot Framework
- Cypress
- BrowserStack

Syllabus
Certified Test Automation Professional (CTAP)
Foundation

Version 1.0

This material contains diagrams and text information based upon:
CTAP, owned by the Certified Test Automation Professional (CTAP) consortium.

Index

Description

This syllabus describes the Certified Test Automation Professional (CTAP) Foundation Level Certification requirements, learning objectives and related information to prepare for the CTAP Foundation exam.

Need for standardized approach in test automation

Professionals and organizations are becoming increasingly dependent on IT, which raises questions about the quality of software.

The speed at which software is developed today makes manual testing obsolete. It's not easy to keep the pace up. The speed of development and releases is important in an Agile/DevOps environment. The concepts of Continuous Integration and Continuous Delivery (CI/CD) are commonplace nowadays. Continuous testing is a need of CI/CD, where test automation plays a key role.

In this scenario, test automation extends beyond simply automating regression tests. Test automation must be implemented across the entire development process. This requires that tests must be administered as quickly as possible and, preferably, automatically.

Test automation is one of the first things that is implemented within Agile teams. However, knowledge and expertise are frequently restricted to one team or project and are difficult to transfer to other teams or projects.

An overly technical approach is frequently suggested, with the main focus on tools and too little attention paid to people, organizations, data and processes. This makes it difficult to scale and transfer best practices within an organization.

The goal is to set up test automation in a way that will be beneficial in the future so that other members of the organization can take advantage of it. Extra attention is required for the creation of test automation that is reusable, expandable, and transferable in such a manner that inside the organization a reliable quality level of test automation is attained.

This demands more attention to detail and a focus on transferability and knowledge sharing, but it also affects how specific test situations and test scripts are created.

Certified Test Automation Professionals and organizations benefit from:

- Increased quality of test automation;
- Reusability of test automation;
- Ability to leverage industry best practice from a vast number of professionals over many years;
- Availability of a common language within your team and organization in relation to test automation;
- Guaranteed quality levels of a test automation engineer.

About the CTAP consortium

The CTAP consortium is a non-for-profit collaboration of industry experts, consultancy organizations, end users, trainers and academics. All these participants believe that the automation of testing involves common approaches that should always be followed, regardless of a professional's background, type of tooling used and industry.

CTAP stands for Certified Test Automation Professional. The shared ambition of the consortium members and its founders is to ensure that professionals who are active within the testing domain have been certified in CTAP, and therefore can benefit from a common understanding of best practice in test automation. The aim is to also ensure a proper execution, enabling higher quality software and reusability of test automation. The Foundation level is the first level which is completed. Applying the CTAP accreditation will guarantee an assured quality level of test automation engineers.

The CTAP consortium has set out three main activity areas through which to achieve this goal:

1. Auditing the supported Test Automation Certification and trainer accreditation program.
2. Promoting the adoption of test automation in public and private organizations.
3. Facilitating access to test automation learning materials and certification for individuals who want to increase their employability.

The Certification Council is an independent panel of test automation and certification experts, each representing different industries and interests. Council members are selected from member organizations of the CTAP consortium based on their experience, network and contributions to test automation.

The Council provides advice on content-related matters and is responsible for auditing the Test Automation Certification based on market standards.

The ambition of the CTAP consortium is to:

"Create a common understanding of the level of expertise required for managing test automation."

Practical information

You must pass a multiple-choice exam in which your knowledge of test automation will be assessed to obtain the CTAP certificate.

All exam candidates will get access to the online exam environment and will need to answer 40 multiple-choice questions within 60 minutes.

You must answer 65% of the questions correctly (or at least 39 of the 60 questions) in order to pass. Each question usually has four possible answers and only one of these is the best answer.

You will receive the result immediately after the exam. (Digital) Access to your certificate will be given once you have passed.

Registration for the exam can be done by purchasing a participation certificate at www.vhls.global.

Number of questions:	40
Time (minutes) for the exam:	60 minutes
% minimal passing grade	65%
Open/closed book:	Closed
Language:	Dutch and English. See www.vhls.global for other available languages.
Exam format:	Online
Type of questions:	Multiple choice. Candidates are advised to read the questions carefully.
Are there also negative questions included in the exam?	Yes. Candidates are advised to read the questions carefully.

Levels

The Certified Test Automation Professional (CTAP) Foundation Certification tests candidates at levels 1 and 2, according to the Bloom Revised Taxonomy.

Bloom Level 1: Recall & Retention

We test candidates on their ability to memorize factual information, to retain information by collecting, remembering and recognizing specific knowledge. Knowledge includes facts, terms, answers or terminology.

Bloom Level 2: Understanding
We test candidates on their ability to construct meaning from oral, written or graphical pieces of information. This is done by interpreting, summarizing, distracting, comparing, classifying, predicting or explaining the message.

Learning objectives

The learning objectives state what the delegate will need to know and be able to execute after successfully obtaining this certification. The certificate that the student will receive proves that they have learned:

- An understanding of test automation.
- Why test automation is important for current development methods.
- What are the purposes of test automation.
- The advantages and disadvantages of test automation.
- In which cases are test automation applicable.
- Which trends are recognized inside test automation.
- Different kinds of test tools.
- Selection of test tools.
- The evolution of test automation.
- Manual vs automated testing.
- Scripting.
- Implementation of test tooling.
- Future-proof development of test automation.
- Introduction to scripting.
- Testing automation and development methods.
- Testing automation functions.
- A CTAP certified person is able to implement test automation inside an Agile release train and to transfer knowledge inside and outside the release train.

Exam requirements and specifications

Module	Exam Requirements	Exam Specification	Weight %	Ref.
1	Introduction		10%	
1.1		The importance of test automation for current development methods		A, D
1.2		The purposes of test automation		D
1.3		Advantages and disadvantages of test automation		D
1.4		A CTAP certified person is able to implement test automation inside an Agile release train and to transfer knowledge inside and outside the release train		B, D
2	Test automation		30%	
2.1		The cases in which test automation is applicable		D, H
2.2		Which trends are recognized inside test automation		D
3	Tooling & Scripting		35%	
3.1		Different kinds of test tools		D
3.2		Selection of test tools		D
3.3		Introduction to scripting		D
3.4		Implementation of test tooling		D
3.5		Scripting		D
4	Establishment of test automation		10%	
4.1		The evolution of test automation		A
5	Architecture		15%	
5.1		Manual vs automated testing		A
5.2		Future-proof development of test automation		A
5.3		Test automation and development methods		A
5.4		Test automation functions		A

Key terms and concepts

The following terms are relevant to the CTAP certification

Definition	Description
Agile	Agile simply means continuous incremental improvement through small and frequent releases and collaboration.
Architecture	A description of a system from different perspectives for the purpose of guiding the design and evolution of the system.
Architecture principle	Statement that expresses a belief and gives direction to the design of one or more systems.
Record & playback tool	A tool that takes input during manual test execution to generate test scripts that can later be automatically executed.
Data generation	The process of defining the test data for an application to be tested.
Data-driven testing	A form of testing in which test cases use test data (input and output) defined in a separate file.
DevOps	Integrating software development and operations so that responsibility for the entire lifecycle falls under the responsibility of one team.
Driver	A software component that calls and/or controls other software components.
Dynamic test	A test in which the program code of the system under test is executed.
Feature	The product's service/function that provides business value and meets customer needs.
Functional test	A test based on the functional requirements.
Event driven testing	A form of testing in which test cases are defined (recorded) in terms of the events that occur when using the system under test.
Behavior driven testing	A form of testing in which test cases are expressed in a pseudo language in terms of Given-When-Then, that is close to natural language.
Reusability	The reuse of developed automated components in other test levels or test formats.
Repeatability	The repeated execution of automated tests without significant adjustments.
Keyword driven testing	Testing based on test cases expressed in keywords, where the keywords are expressed in actions to be performed.

Model driven testing	A form of testing in which the test cases are expressed in structured models that can be interpreted automatically.
Non-functional test	A test based on the quality requirements with regard to non-functional requirements such as Performance testing.
DTAP	Development- Test- Acceptance- Production- environments.
Transferability	Transferring automated tests to users other than the original test engineer or other technology.
Perspective	A way of looking at reality.
Production data	Data as present in the production environment.
Regression test	Testing a previously tested software component after a change to determine that no bugs have been introduced or disclosed in unmodified areas of the software component as a result of those changes.
Stub	A minimal implementation of a software component, used to develop or test a component that calls or otherwise depends on that software component.
Synthetic test data	Data generated specifically for testing purposes.
Static test	A review or inspection of documentation or program code
Test analyst	The person who defines tests on a functional level.
Test architect	The person who draws up the contours of the test project.
Test automation	Using software to perform or support testing activities.
Test automation framework	A set of software components that can be used in programming automated tests, including agreements on their use.
Testing policy	Laying down the most important principles about how testing and test automation are handled. Indicating how test automation is organized in an organizational way.
Test consultant	The person who advises the project and line organization on test vision and policy.
Test data	Data that is needed for a test to work or that arises during the execution of a test.
Test data engineer	The person who ensures that the required test data is made available in any way that complies with regular laws and regulations.
Test data management	Ensuring that good test data is available to support the testing process

Test data strategy	The approach and elaboration of how an organization deals with the use of test data, the development and management of the use of test data.
Test engineer	The person who defines tests on a technical level.
Test management	Planning, budgeting, monitoring and controlling test activities.
Test run	The execution of one or more test cases on the system to be tested.
Test level	A group of testing activities that are jointly organized and managed. A test level is linked to the responsibilities in a project such as unit test, system test, functional acceptance test, e2e test, user acceptance test and production acceptance test.
Test suite	A collection of test cases that belong together.
Test tool	A computer program that supports one or more test activities such as planning and management, specifying, building initial files and data, running the test, and test analysis.
Test performer	The person who performs the defined tests.
Test vision	Describing the objectives of test automation within an organization.
Test type	A collection of test activities with the objective of testing a component or application on one or more related quality attributes such as a functional test, a performance test or a security test.
Test ware	Those products that are made to carry out the test process, such as a test plan, test cases, test scripts and test data.
Velocity	The speed of a development process, typically expressed in the number of user stories completed and tested per iteration.
Virtualization	Creating an environment to simulate hardware functionality within software is run.

Recommended literature

ID.	Source	Form
[A]	'Testautomatisering wendbaar organiseren' – Rooyen, van J, Mersie, MJ, – 2020	Core literature
D	Geautomatiseerd software testen. Egbert Bouman	Core litrature
H	M. Siteur: "Automate your testing, sleep while you are working, blz 143-144," Academic Service, 2005.	Core literature
B	'Het gebruik van testautomatisering binnen Agile projecten' – Rooyen, van J – 2012	Optional
C	'Acht redenen om te beginnen met unit tests' – https://www.delta-n.nl	Optional
E	D. Greefhorst, M. Mersie, J. van Rooyen: "Principes van testautomatisering," Computable, 2015.	Optional
F	J. van Rooyen: "Effort estimation test automation in an Agile environment," Valid2016, 2016.	Optional
G	C. Schotanus et al.: "Testframe, hoofdstuk 6,7,8," Academic Service, 2008.	Optional
I	J. van Rooyen: "Het gebruik van testautomatisering binnen Agile projecten", 2012.	Optional
J	Ravichandran et al.: "DevOps for Digital Leaders" CA Press, 2016	Optional

[redacted]

SLIDE DECK

[redacted]

Program

- **Day 1**
- Test tool overview
- Working with:
  - Graphical user interface
  - Programming interface
- Test tool selection
  - Tool adoption
  - Tool selection
- Working with:
  - Graphical user interface
  - Robot Framework

Program

Day 2

- Test roles
- Continuous testing
- Working with:
  - Robot Framework
  - Cypress
  - BrowserStack

2

Program

Day 2

- Test roles
- Continuous testing
- Working with:
  - Robot Framework
  - Cypress
  - BrowserStack

 3

The group

- Be open
- Be critical
- Be involved

 4

Announcements

- Time
- Breaks/lunch
- Disruptions: mobile phones
- Questions asked?
- Materials

 5

Materials

- Courseware
- Exercises
- Tools:
  - Selenium IDE plug-in
  - Postman
  - Robot Framework
    - Python
  - Cypress
    - Nodejs
  - Visual Studio Code

 6

Introduction – let's get acquainted

- Which tools do you use?
- Nothing yet?
  Choose the tool that best fits your wishes
- There are tools available for every budget
- It is important to determine in advance what you are going to test

7

Test tool overview

In the last couple of years the number of test tools has increased enormously

© Van Haren Publishing BV. 9

What is test automation?

Test automation is that part of the test where you can use tools

Differences between test automation and automated testing

- *Automated testing (test execution)*:
  - By this we mean the automated execution of test cases, test scripts and results assessment
    - It has been recognized this can done be better by computers than by hand
- *Test automation (in general)*:
  - Test automation not only includes *test execution*, but also the automated support of all different proccesses within testing, such as:
    - Test design / Test analysis
    - Test management tools
      - saving test cases
      - registering and *monitoring* findings
    - Test environment, test data tools

© Van Haren Publishing BV. 10

Differences between test automation and automated testing

- ***Automated testing (test execution)*:**
  - By this we mean the automated execution of test cases, test scripts and results assessment
    - It has been recognized this can done be better by computers than by hand
- ***Test automation (in general)*:**
  - Test automation not only includes *test execution*, but also the automated support of all different proccesses within testing, such as:
    - Test design / Test analysis
    - Test management tools
      - saving test cases
      - registering and *monitoring* findings
    - Test environment, test data tools

 11

Examples of test automation: test mgt tools

GitLab
SMARTBEAR Zephyr Enterprise
mockaroo
Bitbucket
qTest Tricentis
TestRail
Testnummers.nl
mantis BUG TRACKER
opentext ALM Quality Center
curiosity
DATPROF
Subsetten & Anonimiseren
Bugzilla
Quality Center
Application Lifecycle Management
JIRA
Xray
mcdc_gen.exe
pairwiseTool
FAKE NAME GENERATOR™
Faker
TESTMONITOR

 12

Examples of test automation: test execution tools

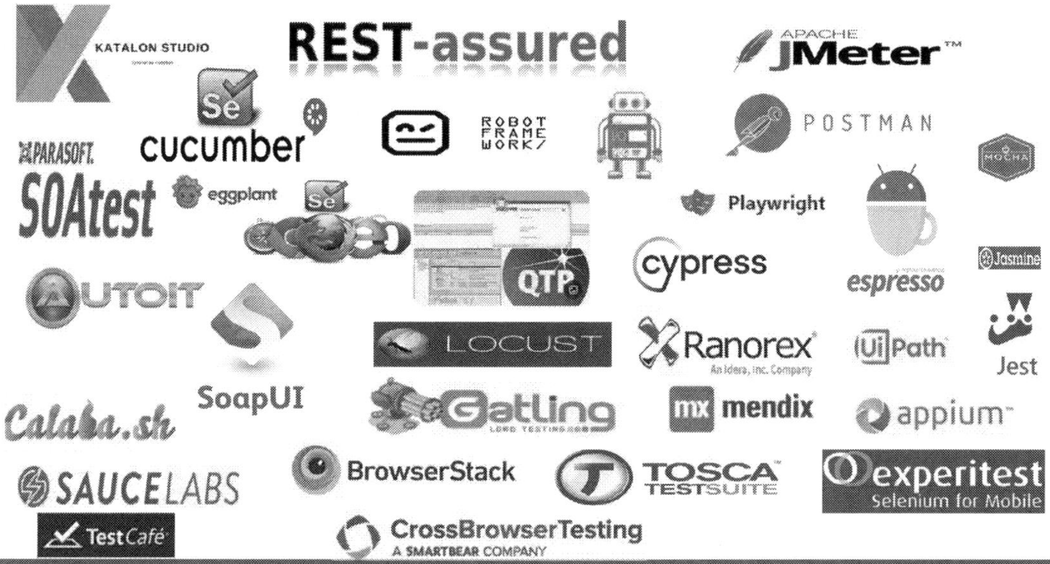

 13

Why automated testing?

- Reasons:
  - *I don't want to do the same thing over and over*
  - *I want testing to run while I am asleep*
  - *I want regression testing*
  - *I want performance testing*
  - *Because it's fun!*

 14

Why automated testing?

- When testing, repeatedly performing the same tests and checks plays an essential role
- For example: when re-testing to assess whether a finding has been resolved, or when performing regression tests

 15

Automated testing becomes more important

- Due to the increasing need for shorter time-to-market
- By applying the Agile/Scrum method (incremental development of products)
- Through *DevOps* (Continuous Integration and Continuous Delivery)

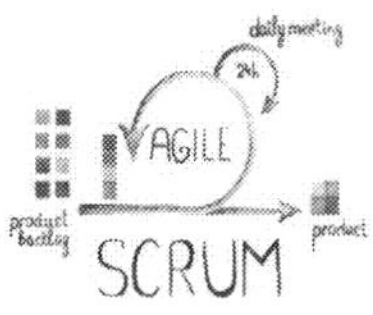

 16

Goals of automated testing

- Increasing and rebuilding the functional coverage
- Reducing test costs
- Performing tests that can't be performed manually (security tests, performance tests)
- Shortening the lead time of test execution
- Realizing a faster feedback of test results

Benefits of automated testing

- *Speed: tools are faster than humans*
- *Repeatable: tools can perform exactly the same actions again and again*
- *Re-usable: on different versions of software*
- *Manageable: think of test design, test scripts, assessment management*

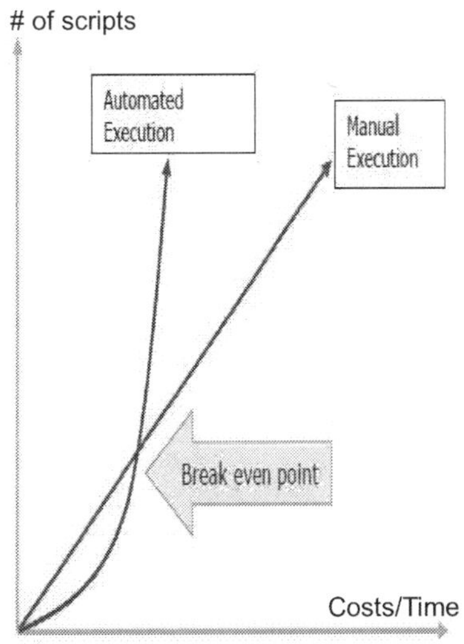

Why not start right away?

Counter arguments

- Tooling requires the necessary expertise
- License costs

- Not every test script can be used multiple times

- Maintenance of test scripts
- Application is subject to too much change

- Creating a good test environment takes a lot of time and is expensive

Arguments in favor

- Higher reliability by switching off the human factor
- Higher productivity allowing more test to be performed
- More job satisfaction due to automating routine activities

 21

Arguments in favor

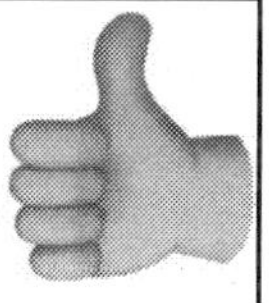

More testing options, for example:

performance- security- and *regression testing*

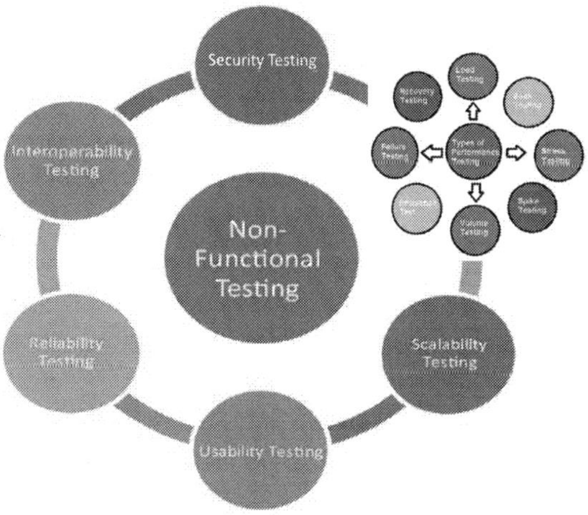

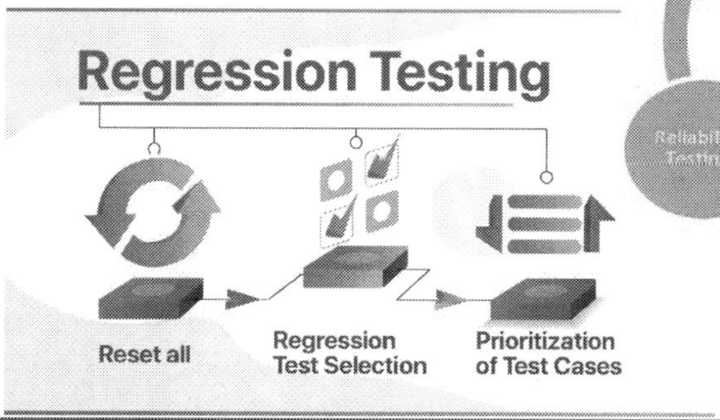

 22

Arguments in favor

- Reducing test time helps to enhance customer service
- Finding errors earlier:
  - Reduces the number of production incidents
  - Helps by reducing error recovery costs
- The use of a tool forces a standard way of working

 23

When can you start?

- The stability of the code
  - Are there not many more changes in the part of the application where you want to automate testing?

  >> Then you are ready to start!

 24

When can you start?

- The maturity of your test organization
  - Do you have a test environment? Do the testers work in a uniform manner?

  >> Then you are ready to start!

 25

When can you start?

- The objective of your organization
  - As an organization, do you want a quicker time-to-market or more releases per year?

  >> Perhaps you are ready to automate testing

 26

It only makes sense if

- Automating a test only makes sense if you are able to perform a test manually
- If you know the chronological steps and can *script* the test case, then test automation is a logical next step
- *Scripted testing* is usually a "non-thinking activity" where testers perform the test steps and compare actual results with expected results
- Such test execution can be automated and does not require much cognitive skills
- Preferably suitable for regression or performance testing

 27

Scripted testing

Step	Action	Expected result
1	I'm doing this	and I expect (to see) this
2	Then I do this	and I expect (to see) this
3	...	......

First you determine the (correct) order of actions

Then describe you what the expected result will be

 28

Scripted testing - Exercise - ATM

In pairs, describe in chronological order all the actions that occur when withdrawing money.

One person represents the ATM

The other the pinner.

 29

Working with tools for the graphical user interface

cucumber ROBOT FRAMEWORK APACHE JMeter™ appium Playwright QuickTest Professional KATALON STUDIO Quality Center Application Lifecycle Management Visual Studio AUTOIT Ranorex BrowserStack TOSCA TESTSUITE experitest Selenium for Mobile curiosity cypress TestCafé mendix

COURSEWARE

Test execution

Tools that can automate the test execution are available in several editions, for example:

- Via the graphical user interface
- Via a so-called program interface

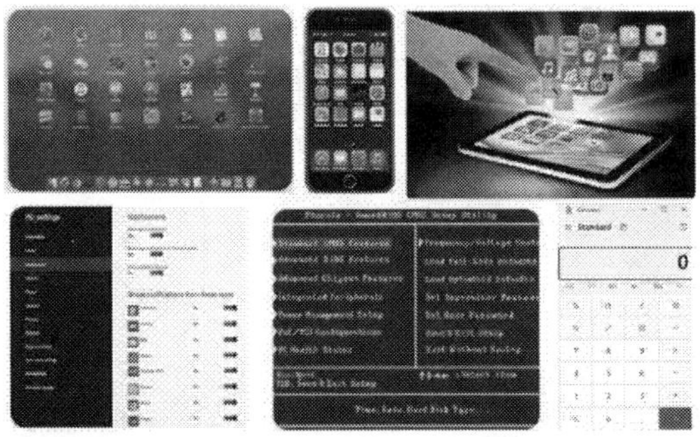

 31

Through the graphical user interface (GUI)

- There are tools which work by recording actions so that they can be replayed
- These are also called *record & playback tools* or *first generation* test tools

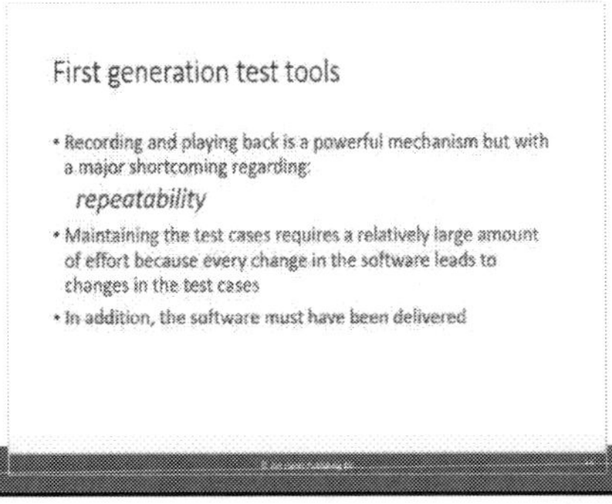
First generation test tools

- Recording and playing back is a powerful mechanism but with a major shortcoming regarding:
  repeatability
- Maintaining the test cases requires a relatively large amount of effort because every change in the software leads to changes in the test cases
- In addition, the software must have been delivered

 32

First generation test tools

- Recording and playing back is a powerful mechanism but with a major shortcoming regarding:

  repeatability
- Maintaining the test cases requires a relatively large amount of effort because every change in the software leads to changes in the test cases
- In addition, the software must have been delivered

Through the graphical user interface (GUI)

- (Open source) examples are:

Selenium IDE
Katalon
TOSCA TESTSUITE
APACHE JMeter™
cypress

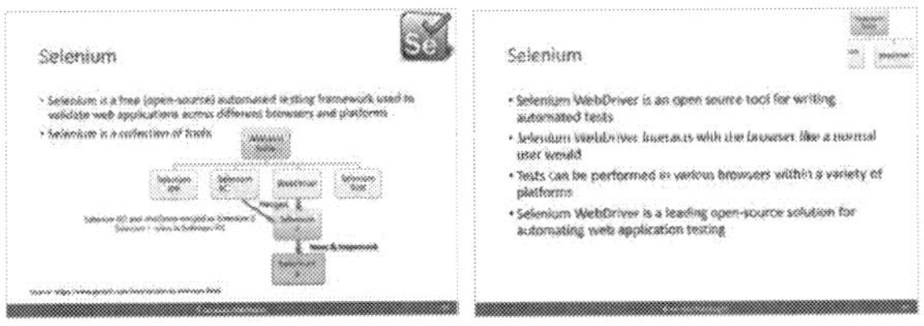

https://www.softwaretestinghelp.com/best-gui-testing-tools/

Selenium

- Selenium is a free (open-source) automated testing framework used to validate web applications across different browsers and platforms
- Selenium is a collection of tools

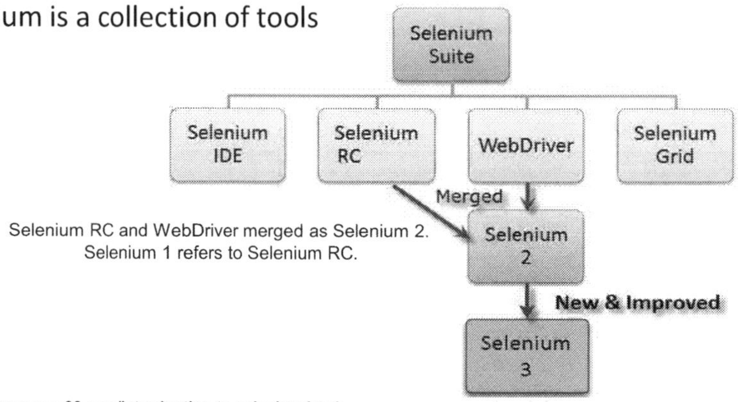

Source: https://www.guru99.com/introduction-to-selenium.html

 35

Selenium

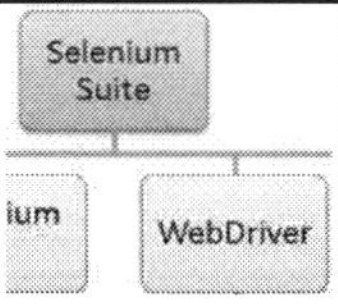

- Selenium WebDriver is an open source tool for writing automated tests
- Selenium WebDriver interacts with the browser like a normal user would
- Tests can be performed in various browsers within a variety of platforms
- Selenium WebDriver is a leading open-source solution for automating web application testing

 36

Selenium

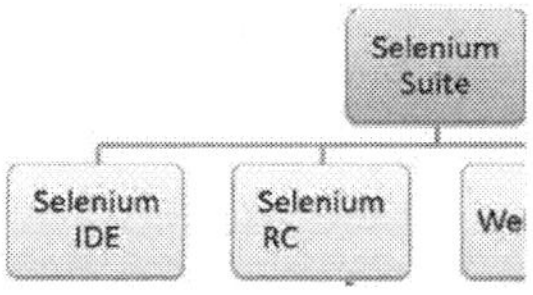

- Selenium IDE, a Chrome/Edge extension that can automate the browser through a record-and-playback feature

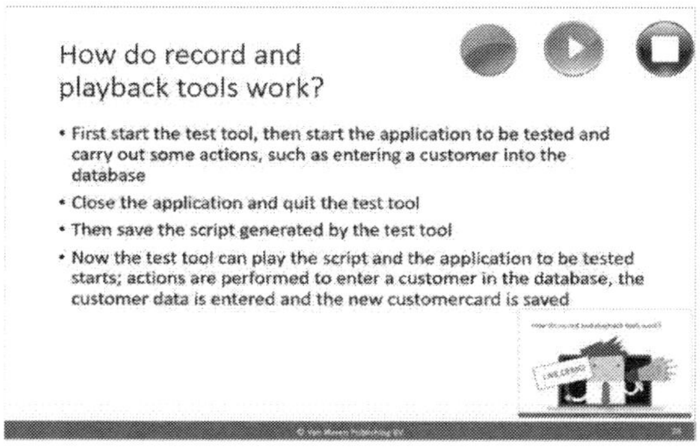

© Van Haren Publishing BV. 37

How do record and playback tools work?

- First start the test tool, then start the application to be tested and carry out some actions, such as entering a customer into the database
- Close the application and quit the test tool
- Then save the script generated by the test tool
- Now the test tool can play the script and the application to be tested starts; actions are performed to enter a customer in the database, the customer data is entered and the new customercard is saved

© Van Haren Publishing BV. 38

How do record and playback tools work?

 40

To work

Exercise:

Open the plug-in in Google Chrome and create a new SAVINGS account. Then make a transfer and check the transfer on the overview page.

Laptop: Welkom01

Userid: *John* Password: *demo*

Url: http://localhost:8080/parabank
Public url: https://parabank.parasoft.com/parabank/index.htm
Hint: Don't forget to log out

 41

When might record and playback be a good option?

- As a learning tool:
  - It can be incredibly useful to record your steps and see what is generated
  - Reviewing these recorded steps can give you real examples of how the underlying automation framework can be leveraged from code

When might record & playback be a good option?

- For load testing:
  - Many load testing tools do record & playback under the hood
  - Testers record test scenarios to capture the requests and responses between the client and server
  - At a very simple level they basically just capture your network traffic and play it back

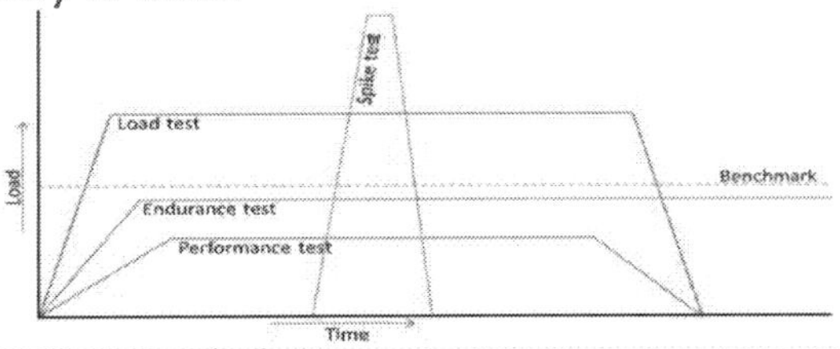

And when not

- Limited test coverage:
  - Record and playback tools perform exactly the steps you have included, possibly including the typos or mis-clicks
  - That means these tests usually don't do much more than basic navigation tests
  - Navigation tests are important, but testing the navigation alone is not enough

 45

2nd Generation

- The *second generation* partly addresses the concerns of *repeatability* where the required input for the test was specified as variables or functions that can be easily adjusted
- For example, by entering a certain age, the route through the system can be different
- This represented an improvement compared to the *first generation*, but was still not ideal

 46

3rd Generation

- In the third generation, test automation became more data-driven
- For example:
    - generating test data,
    - running test scripts and
    - reporting the results
- Despite these developments, it appears difficult to make test automation *future-proof*

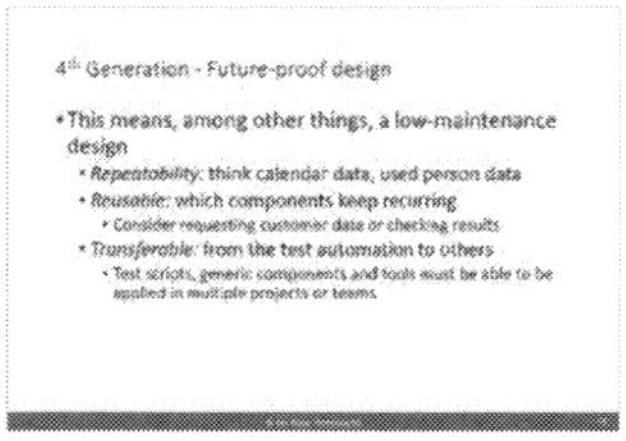

 47

4th Generation - Future-proof design

- This means, among other things, a low-maintenance design
    - *Repeatability:* think calendar data, used person data
    - *Reusable:* which components keep recurring
        - Consider requesting customer data or checking results
    - *Transferable:* from the test automation to others
        - Test scripts, generic components and tools must be able to be applied in multiple projects or teams

 48

5th Generation

Although a 5th generation of test tools already exists, the 4th generation is the starting point for this training because it's most widely used

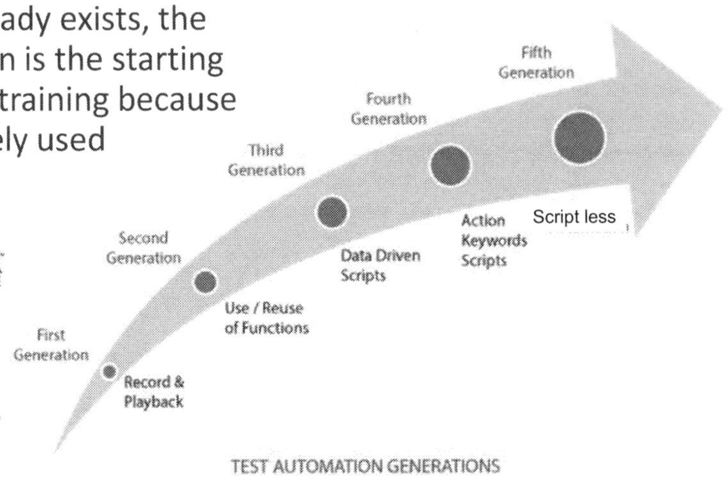

curiosity

© Van Haren Publishing BV 49

curiosity

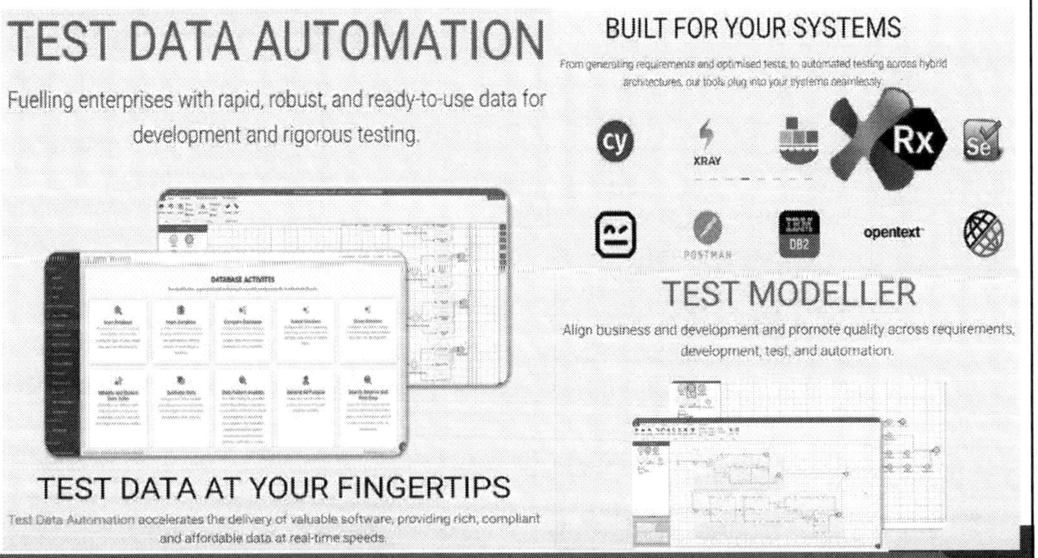

© Van Haren Publishing BV.

- Ranorex is a powerful tool for test automation
- It is a GUI test automation framework used for the testing of web-based, desktop, and mobile applications
- Selenium WebDriver is built into the Ranorex core API
- Ranorex does not have its own scripting language to automate application
- It uses standard programming languages such as VB.NET and C#
- It automates tests on a Windows desktop, then execute locally or remotely on real or virtual machines.

 51

4th Generation

- There are also tools to fully automate the functional actions (*clicking a button on a website or opening an app on a phone*)
- Examples of keyword-driven test tools include:

WebDriver

WebdriverIO

appium

cypress

ROBOT FRAMEWORK

*... like a **mouse click,** selection of a **menu item**, **keystrokes**, **opening** or **closing** a window*

 52

Working with tools through the programming interface

REST-assured

PARASOFT. SOAtest

ROBOT FRAMEWORK

POSTMAN

SoapUI

cypress

Through a programming interface

Tools that can automate the test execution are available in several variants, for example:

- Through the graphical user interface (GUI)
- Through a programming interface (API)

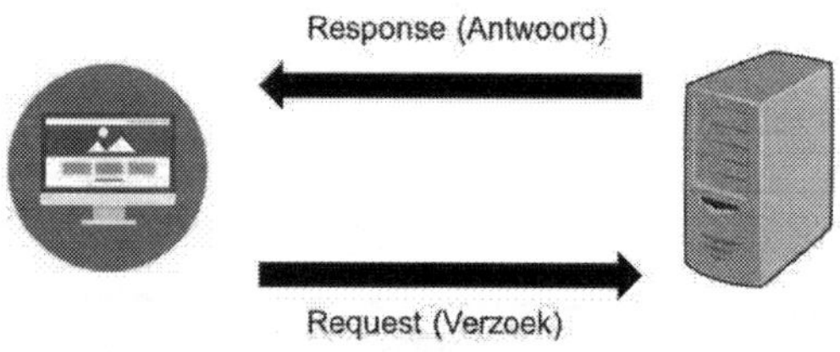

 55

Through a programming interface

- In the context of APIs, the word 'application' refers to any software with a distinct function
- Interface can be thought of as a *contract* of service between two applications
- This *contract* defines how the two communicate with each other using requests and responses

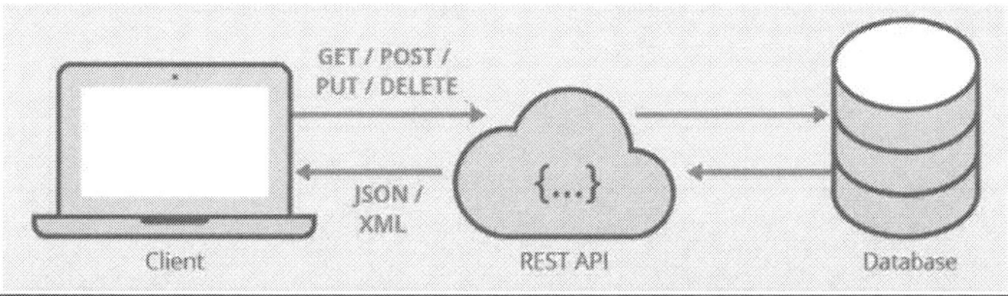

 56

Through a programming interface

- Examples of an *interface* are:
  - Application Programming Interface (API)
  - Messages in XML or JSON format (web service)

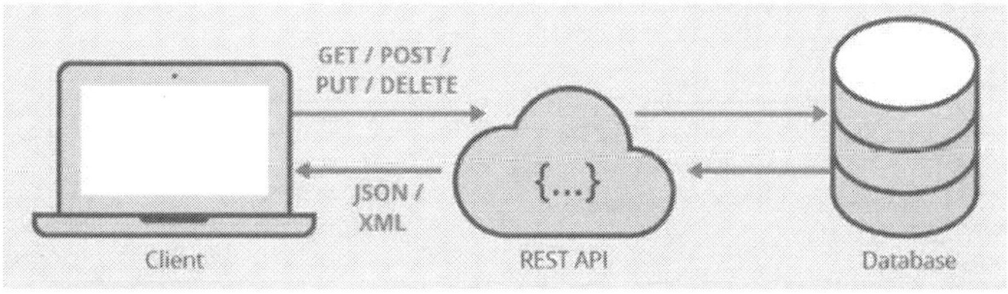

 57

Through a programming interface

- The difference between a web service and an API is in the network
  - *A program interface* that communicates through the internet, based on the SOAP- or REST-protocol, is a *web service*
- *Web services* are made for online machine-to-machine communication
- In fact, it is only the front-end interfaces of websites and applications that reside on end-users' devices
- When it comes to the way the web is made, there are currently two competing approaches: *SOAP* and *REST*

Through a programming interface

- Examples of tools for testing s*ervices*:

SoapUI
PARASOFT. SOAtest
REST-assured
POSTMAN
ROBOT FRAMEWORK
cypress

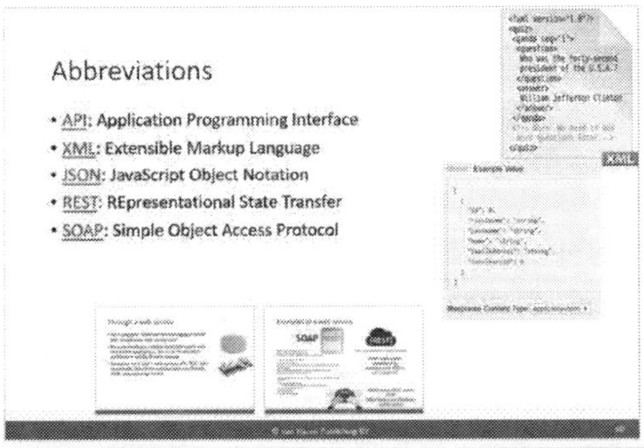

Abbreviations

- API: Application Programming Interface
- XML: Extensible Markup Language
- JSON: JavaScript Object Notation
- REST: REpresentational State Transfer
- SOAP: Simple Object Access Protocol

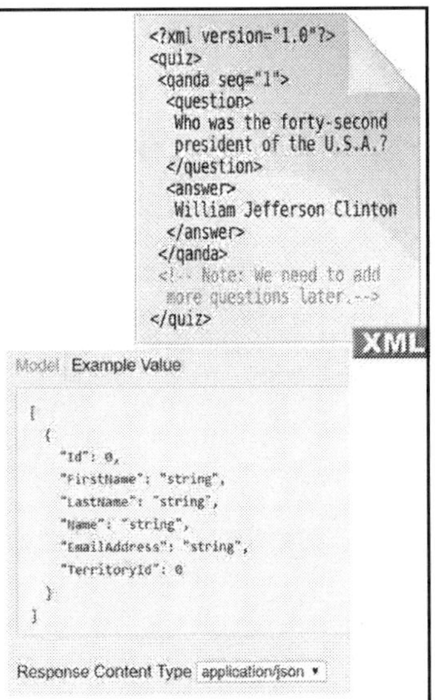

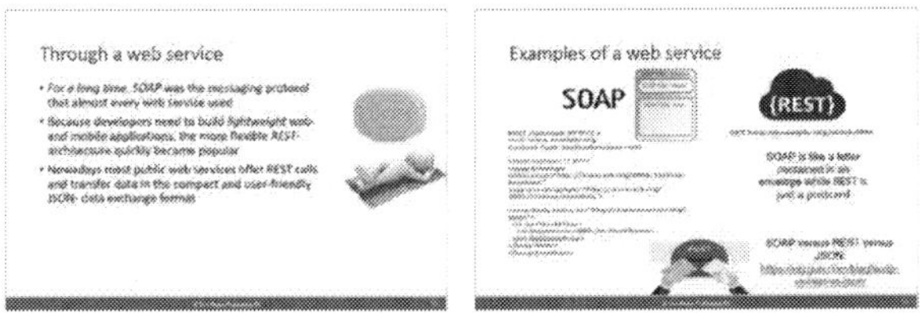

Through a web service

- *For a long time, SOAP* was the messaging protocol that almost every web service used
- Because developers need to build *lightweight* web- and mobile applications, the more flexible *REST*-architecture quickly became popular
- Nowadays most public web services offer REST calls and transfer data in the compact and user-friendly JSON- data exchange format

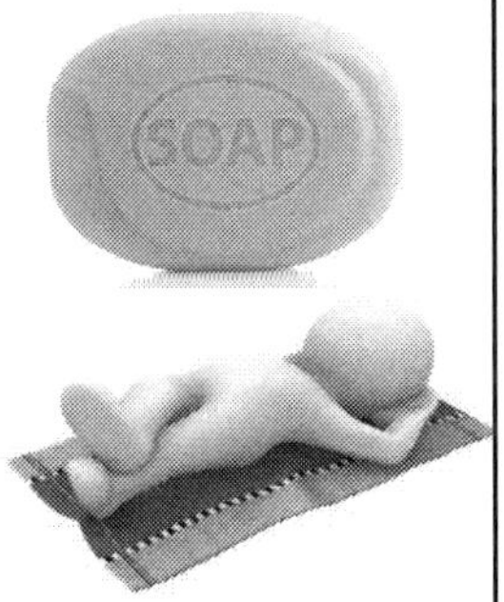

Examples of a web service
SOAP
SOAP-ENV: Envelope
SOAP-ENV: Header
SOAP-ENV: Body
POST /GetStock HTTP/1.1
Host: www.example.org
Content-Type: application/soap+xml
<?xml version="1.0"?>
<soap:Envelope
xmlns:soap="http://www.w3.org/2001/12/soap-envelope"
soap:encodingStyle="http://www.w3.org/2001/12/soap-encoding">
<soap:Body xmlns:m="http://www.example.org/stock">
<m:GetStockPrice>
<m:StockName>IBM</m:StockName>
</m:GetStockPrice>
</soap:Body>
</soap:Envelope>
POST
{REST}
GET http://example.org/stock/IBM
SOAP is like a letter contained in an envelope while REST is just a postcard
SOAP versus REST versus JSON:
https://raygun.com/blog/soap-vs-rest-vs-json/
© Van Haren Publishing BV.
62

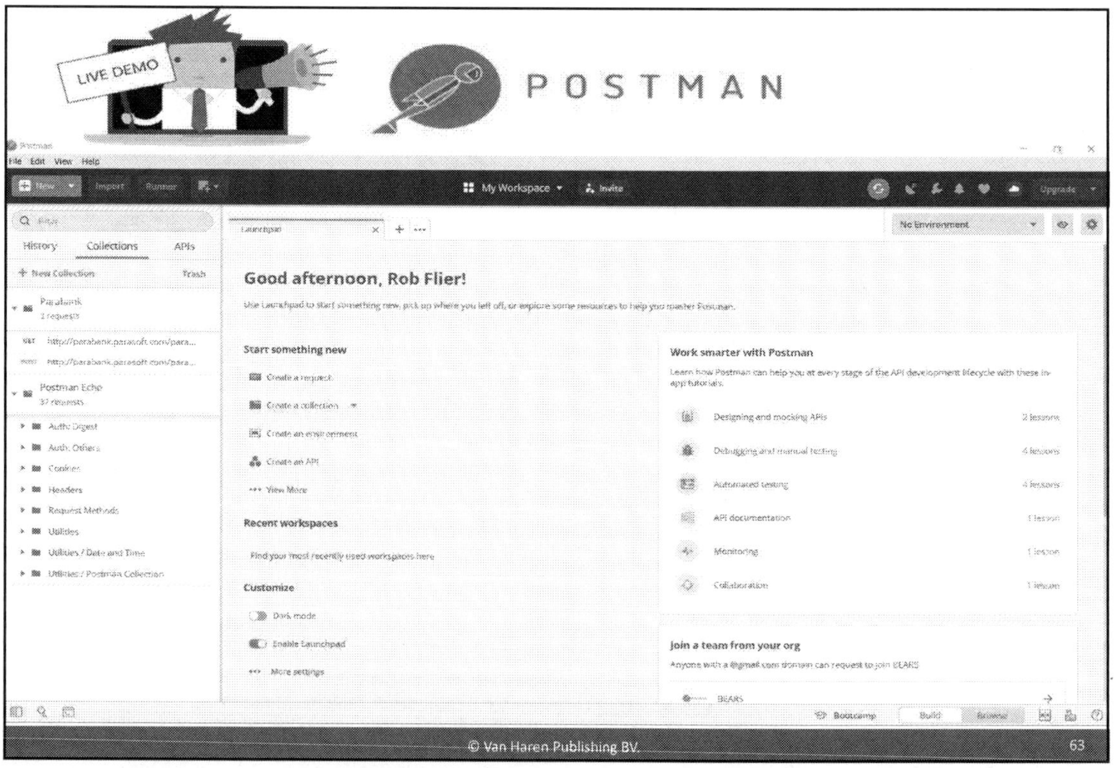
LIVE DEMO
POSTMAN
My Workspace
History
Collections
APIs
Good afternoon, Rob Flier!
Start something new
Work smarter with Postman
Recent workspaces
Customize
Join a team from your org
© Van Haren Publishing BV.
63

Examples of a web service

- http://api.zippopotam.us/us/90210
- Script:

```
<script type="text/javascript"> var client = new XMLHttpRequest(); client.open("GET", "http://api.zippopotam.us/us/90210", true); client.onreadystatechange = function() { if(client.readyState == 4) { alert(client.responseText); }; }; client.send(); </script>
```

Bron: https://zippopotam.us/

Tutorials:

- https://www.guru99.com/postman-tutorial.html
- https://learning.getpostman.com/docs/postman/launching-postman/sending-the-first-request/

 64

Test tool selection

Tool adoption & tool selection

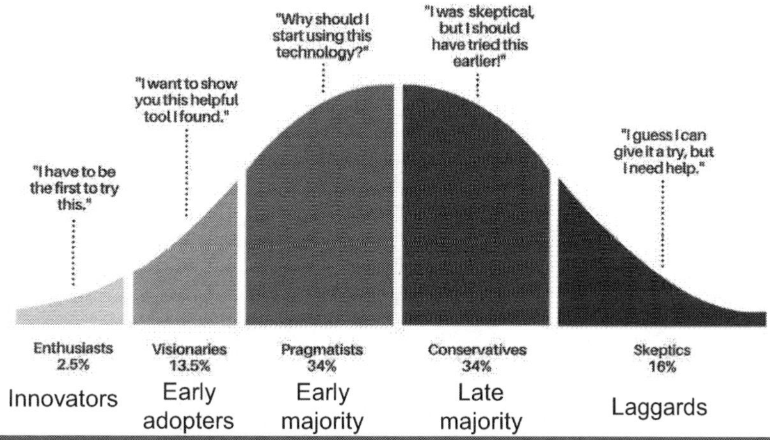

Test tool adoption

- The objectives of test automation and the technical environment are to determine which tools can be used
- A tool selection progress is, therefore, essential for selecting the right tool

COURSEWARE

How to find the right tool?

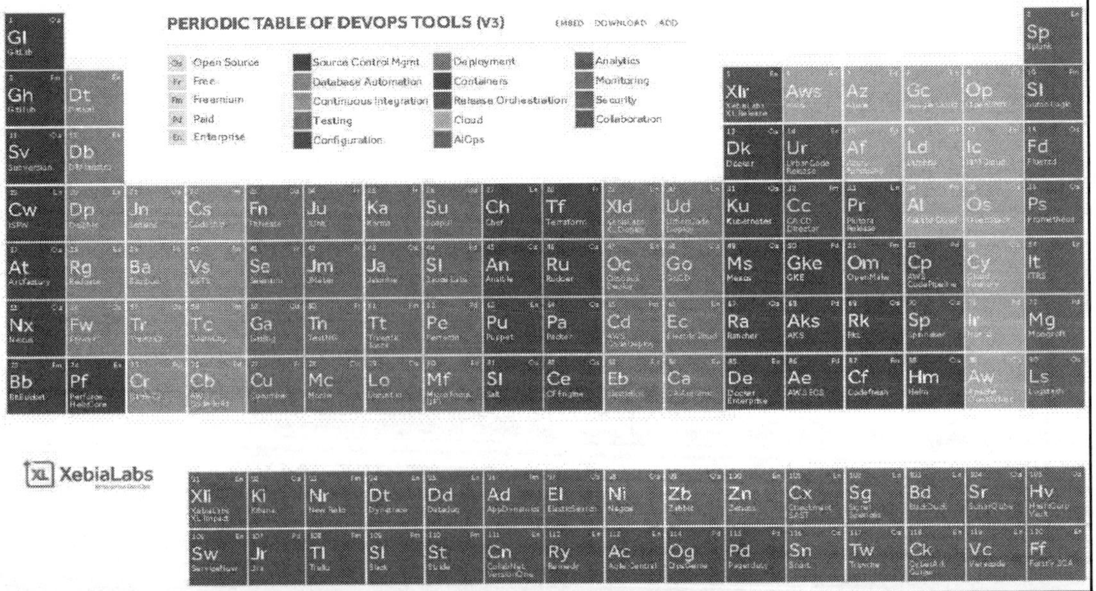

 67

Tool adoption

In practice, one of the following four patterns is almost always evident:

1. The hard-fought success
2. The rapid failure
3. The silent death
4. The smooth success

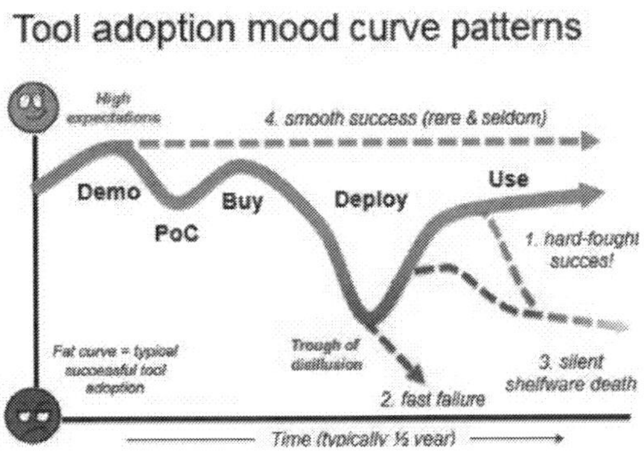

1. The hard-fought success

- Demos are always beautiful and make people happy
- A Proof-of-Concept is more realistic:
  - You actually use the tool in your own situation, with your application, your scripts and your data
  - There are also some disadvantages, so the mood drops a little
- Around the time of purchase everyone is positive again, then the real work begins

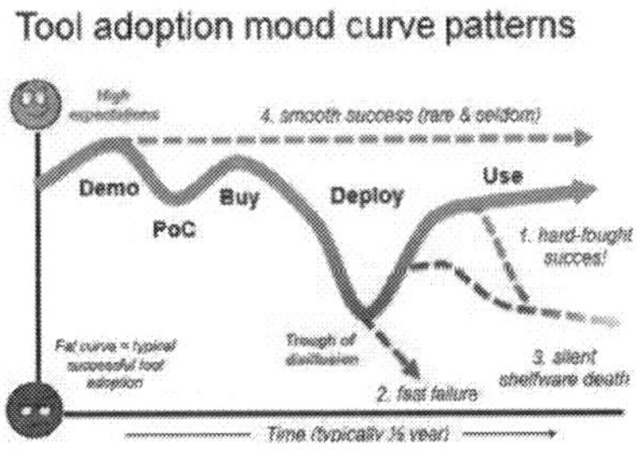

1. The hard-fought success

- Then comes the most dangerous moment: the valley of disillusion:
  - You will almost always have to cross this valley together
  - This is the moment when everyone threatens to lose heart:
    - it turns out to be more difficult than expected, we do not yet have the required knowledge and experience and even worse...
      - the tool contains serious bugs

Tool adoption mood curve patterns

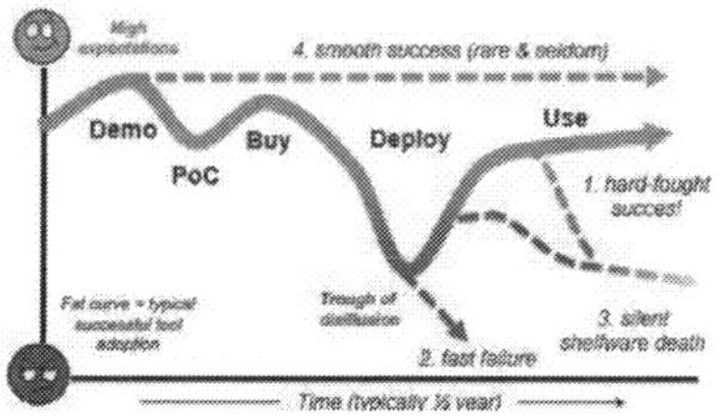

Because, of course, test tools are also software and so they include errors

 70

2. The rapid failure

- What can also become clear in the valley of disillusion is that the choice of tool was an error
- In this case a rapid failure is the cheapest option

Tool adoption mood curve patterns

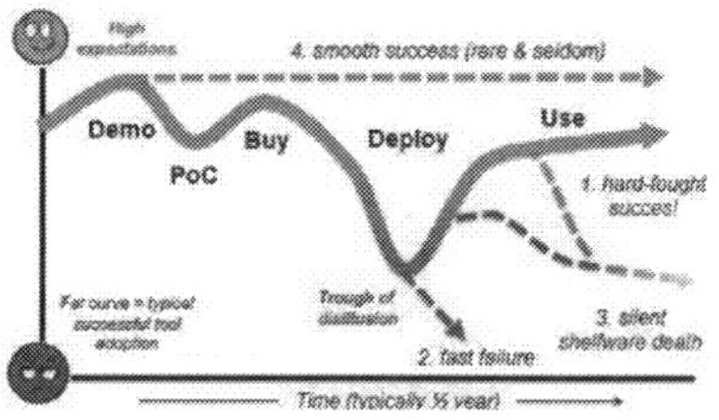

Crying and starting over

 71

3. The silent dead

- They muddle on, things get better and a regression test set starts to work
- But maintaining the scripts proves problematic and the tool slowly disappears into the background

Tool adoption mood curve patterns

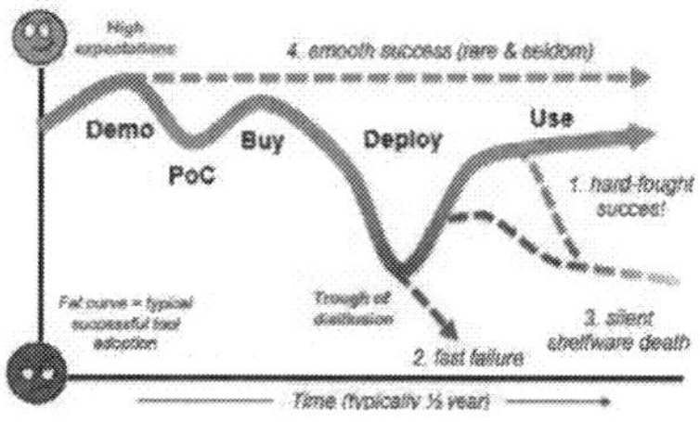

The silent dead is near!

 72

4. The smooth success

- When counting your blessings, also take a look at the future stability and maintainability of the scripts
  - Because in time the problem will usually find itself there

Tool adoption mood curve patterns

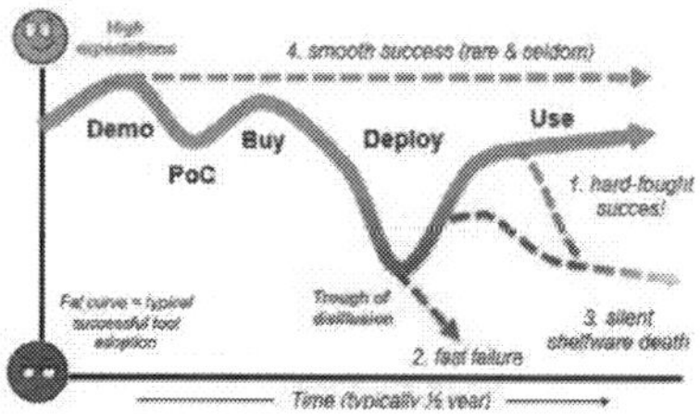

- Knowledge and experience with tool selection and implementation is decisive in recognizing the patterns and making the right decisions at key moments in the process

 73

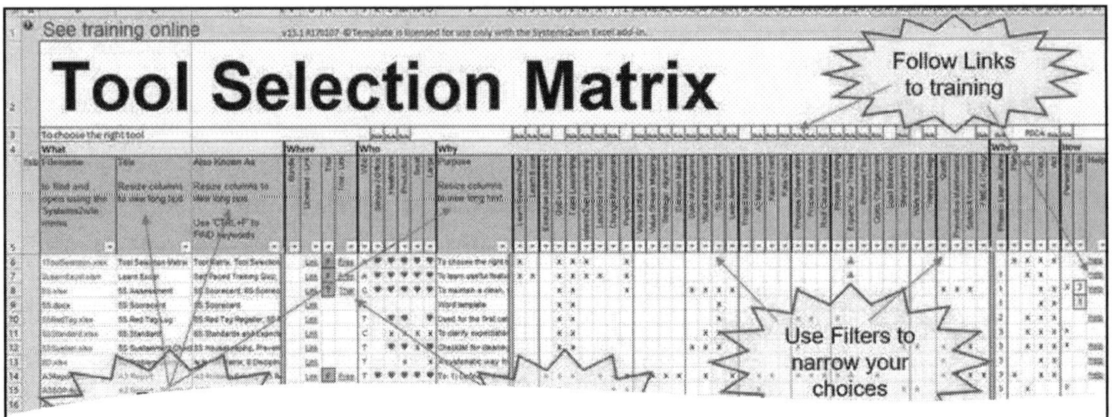

What to consider when choosing a test automation tool

- **Technology Support**: The ability of the tool to support a wide range of technologies and applications should be a primary consideration3: e.g., web, desktop, mobile
- **Scripting or Programming Requirements**: no-code, low-code, full code
- **Open-source vs. Licensed (Pricing)**
- **Ease of Use**
- **Adoption Time**: Time-to-value
- **Customer Support**

© Van Haren Publishing BV. 74

Tool selection

COURSEWARE

© Van Haren Publishing BV.

mx mendix : Low code application

- With Mendix you can develop, deploy, test and manage (mobile) apps from a integrated development environment
- The big advantage is that Mendix is low-code
  - This means that the user can program without having to type a lot of code themselves
- Mendix low-code development supports software development from start to finish

COURSEWARE

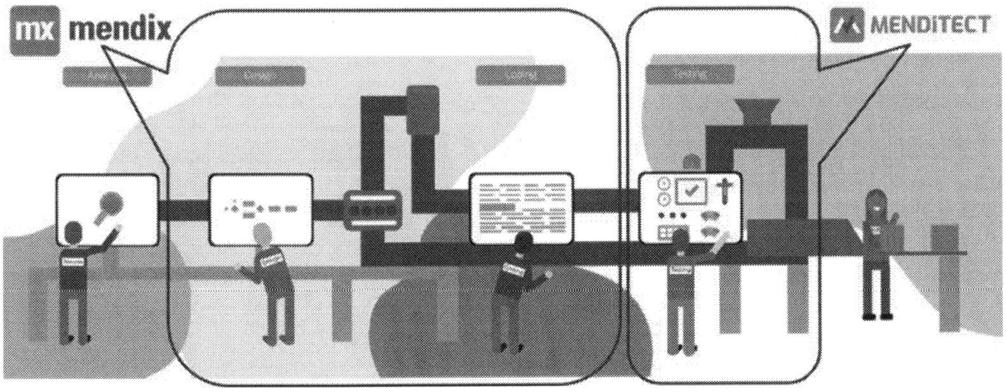

Mendix: Application Test Suite (ATS)

- With ATS, you can automate your functional tests for the user stories you are developing
- These tools are built in Mendix, on top of Selenium
- You do not need any knowledge of Selenium or testing frameworks to write test cases.
- The browser recorder will save every interaction and generate the necessary Selenium scripts

Low code. High impact.

Powered by AI, Mendix is the only low-code platform for complex software development challenges.

Try Mendix for free | Contact Us

 77

Mendix: Application Test Suite (ATS)

- With ATS, you can automate your functional tests for the user stories you are developing
- These tools are built in Mendix, on top of Selenium
- You do not need any knowledge of Selenium or testing frameworks to write test cases.
- The browser recorder will save every interaction and generate the necessary Selenium scripts

Mendix: Application Test Suite (ATS)

- With ATS, you can automate your functional tests for the user stories you are developing
- These tools are built in Mendix, on top of Selenium

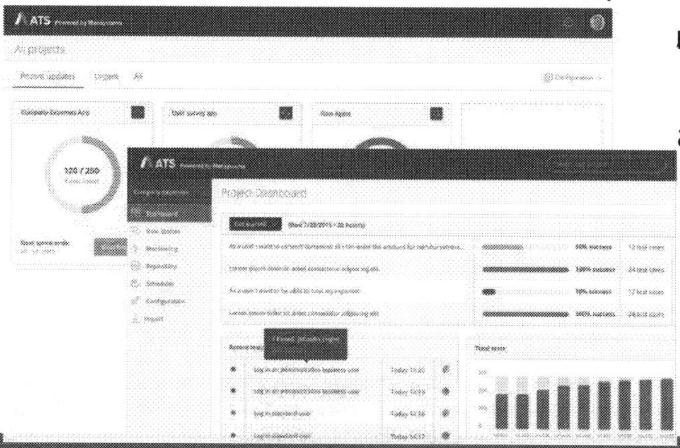

ım or testing

action and generate

What is Selenium WebDriver?

- Selenium WebDriver is a web framework that permits you to execute cross-browser tests
- This tool is used for automating web-based application testing to verify that it performs as expected
- WebDriver drives a browser natively, as a user would
- Selenium WebDriver allows you to choose a programming language to create test scripts

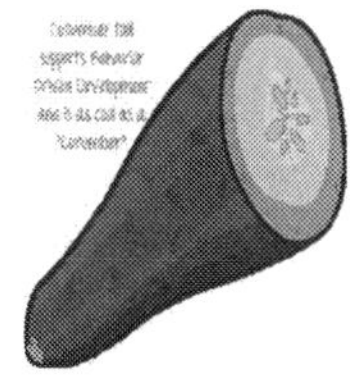

 80

Selenium WebDriver & Cucumber

- Behavior-driven development is a way of working and, especially, thinking about which behavior of the end user is central:
  - The developer together with the tester and PO define the test set for the functionality to be developed
  - After defining the test set, the developer must include the test set in the unit test before the functionality is built
  - The test will fail as the functionality is not yet built
  - After this step, the developer will build the functionality so that the test passes

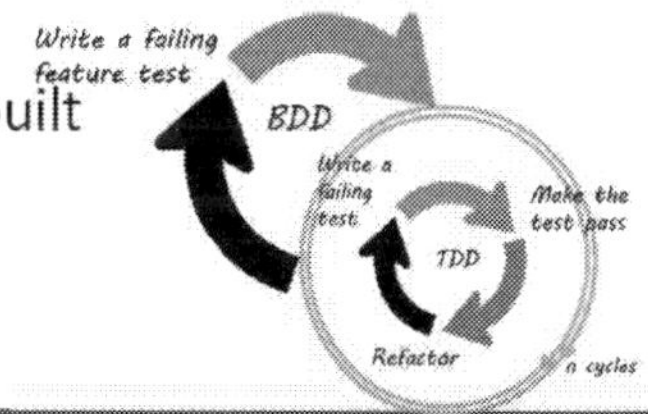

 81

How does Cucumber work?

- Cucumber works differently from other automated tests
    - However, the test automation itself is done by another tool, *Selenium*
- Furthermore, another programming language is used, namely *Gherkin*
- The special thing about *Gherkin* is that this language is actually not extensive at all:
    - In fact, the associated vocabulary is no more than a handful of words

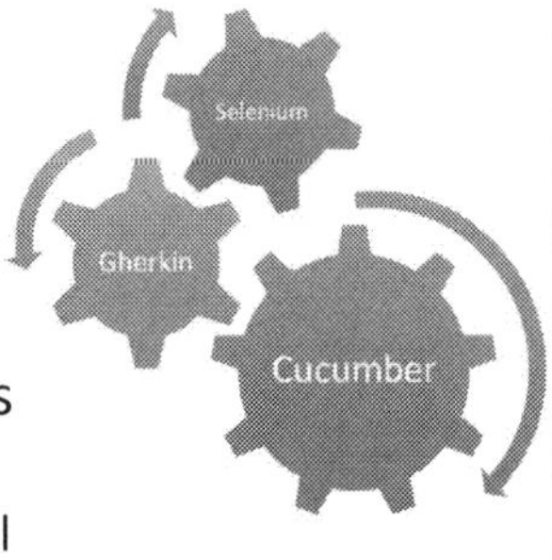

https://cucumber.io/docs/guides/overview/

Gherkin syntax

- *Gherkin* describes the behavior of a system using the syntax *Given, When, Then*
    - The *Given* describes the initial situation
    - The *When* describes the action
    - The *Then* describes the result

```
Feature: A demonstration

  Scenario Outline: Eating

    Given that there are <start> cucumbers
     When I eat <eat> cucumbers
     Then I should have <left> cucumbers

      | start | eat | left |
      | 20    | 10  | 10   |
      | 15    | 3   | 12   |
```

- If there are multiple starting situations, actions or results, the AND can be used
- If you want to make it clear that certain things should not be present, use the BUT

Advantages of Gherkin

- All team members speak the same language, which reduces the risk of miscommunication
- Developers can easily convert the test cases to unit tests while maintaining the Gherkin syntax
- System requirements can be written directly in Gherkin style, because the way of writing is understandable for all team members, but also for the business
- An additional advantage is that Cucumber works relatively quickly: setting up Gherkin-style test cases saves time

https://blog.testfort.com/functional-testing/gherkin-other-approach

What is WebdriverIO?

- It is a next-gen browser and mobile automation test framework for node.js
- WebdriverIO can be run on the Selenium WebDriver Protocol for true cross-browser testing as well as Chrome DevTools Protocol for Chromium-based automation

Working with tools for the graphical user interface

- Robot Framework

COURSEWARE

The case for Robot Framework

- In addition to being free (of charge), Robot Framework has:
  - *Really easy syntax,*
  - *Human-readable keywords*
- Its capabilities can be extended by *libraries* implemented with Python or Java(Script), or any other language
- Robot Framework project is *hosted on GitHub* where you can find further documentation and source code

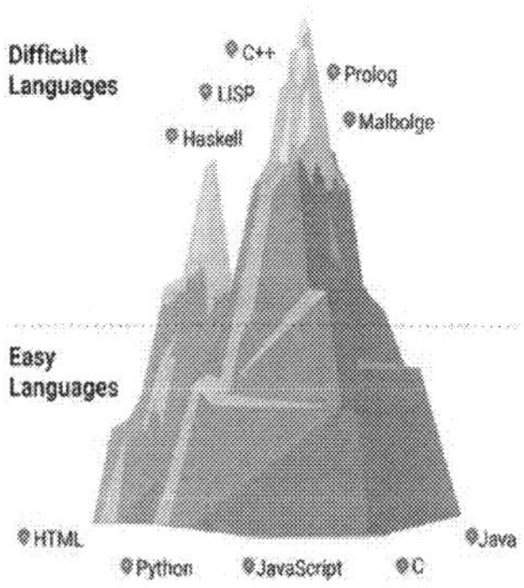

git GitHub

 87

Robot Framework

ROBOT FRAMEWORK

- Robot Framework is a generic open source automation framework
- Being open source also means that Robot Framework is free to use without licensing costs
    - The framework was initially developed at Nokia Networks and was open sourced in 2008

 88

Architecture

ROBOT FRAMEWORK

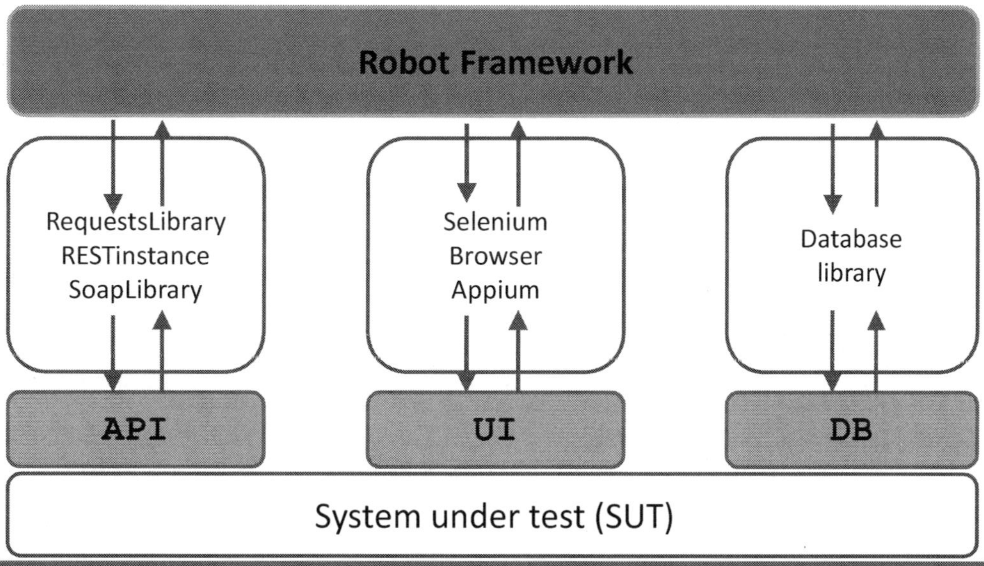

 89

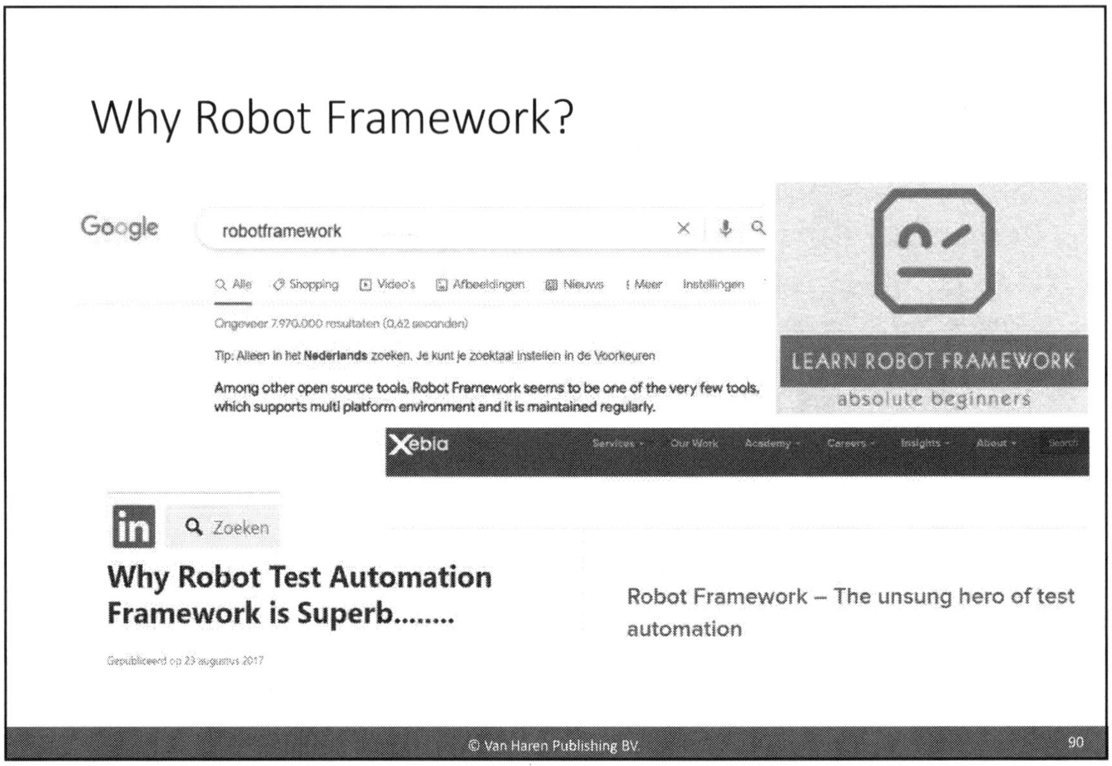
Why Robot Framework?
Google
robotframework
Alle
Shopping
Video's
Afbeeldingen
Nieuws
Meer
Instellingen
Ongeveer 7.970.000 resultaten (0,62 seconden)
Tip: Alleen in het Nederlands zoeken. Je kunt je zoektaal instellen in de Voorkeuren
Among other open source tools, Robot Framework seems to be one of the very few tools, which supports multi platform environment and it is maintained regularly.
LEARN ROBOT FRAMEWORK
absolute beginners
Xebia
Services
Our Work
Academy
Careers
Insights
About
Zoeken
Why Robot Test Automation Framework is Superb........
Gepubliceerd op 23 augustus 2017
Robot Framework – The unsung hero of test automation
© Van Haren Publishing BV.
90

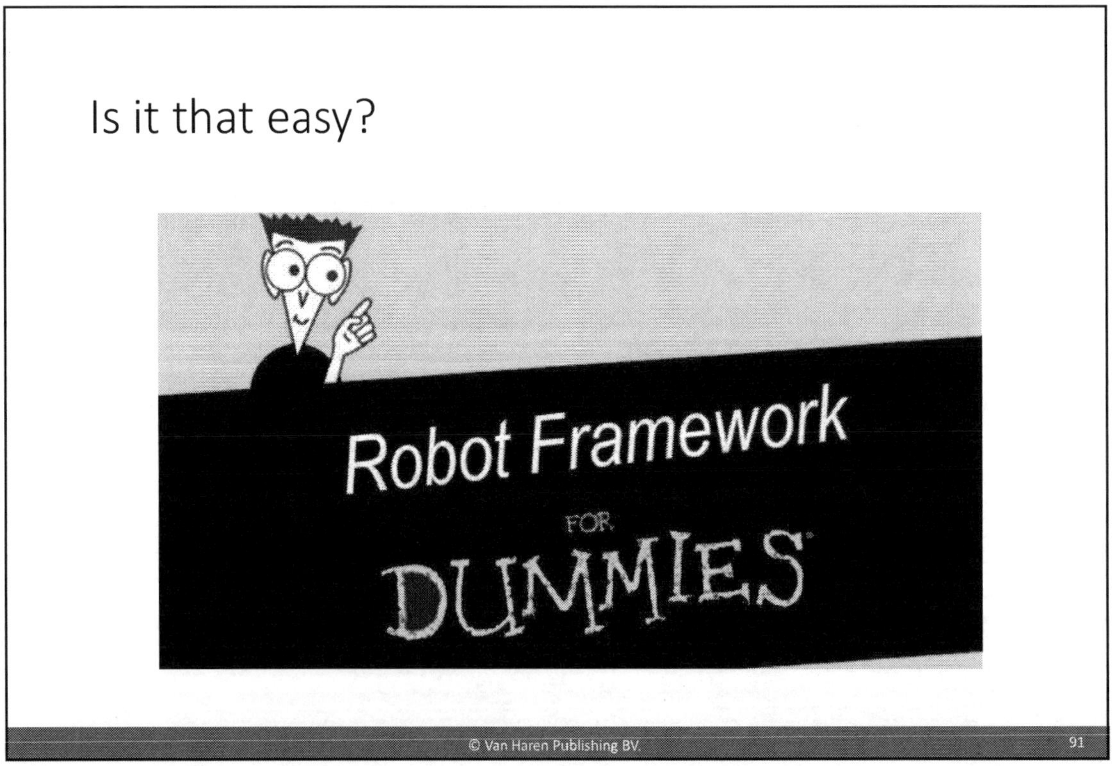
Is it that easy?
Robot Framework
FOR
DUMMIES
© Van Haren Publishing BV.
91

Keywords

- In keyword-driven testing, you first identify a set of keywords and then associate an action (or function) related to these keywords
- Here, every testing action like opening or closing of browser, mouse click, keystrokes, etc. is described by a keyword such as:

  Open Browser https://www.google.com/
  Click Button
  Click Link
  Close Browser

 92

Keywords

Open Browser https://www.google.com/

Input

Click Button

Click Link

 93

Keywords

Open Browser https://www.google.com/

Input

Click Button

Click Link

Close Browser

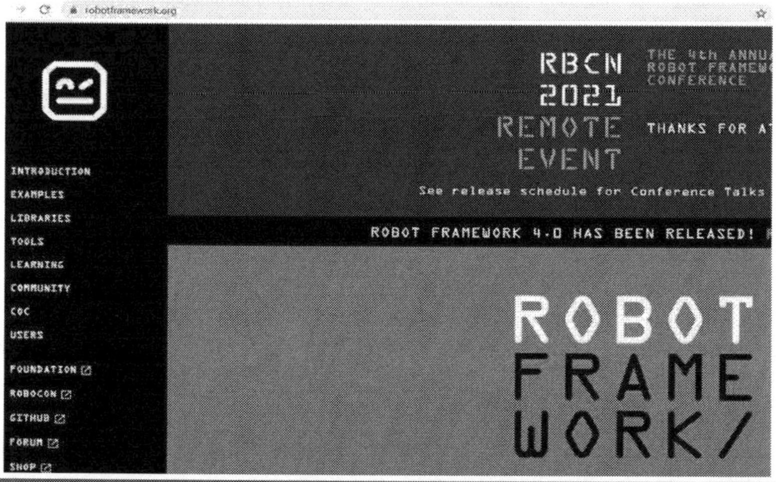

 94

Robot Framework

- Test execution is initiated from the *command prompt / command line / CLI*
    - *Although there is a Robot Framework IDE called RIDE*
- As a result, you will get a report in both HTML format and XML output

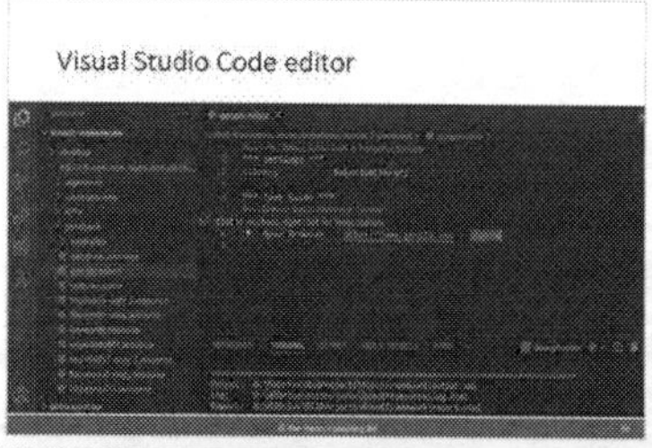

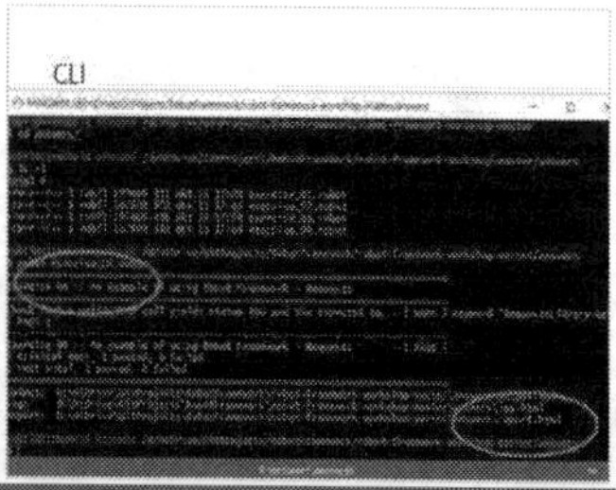

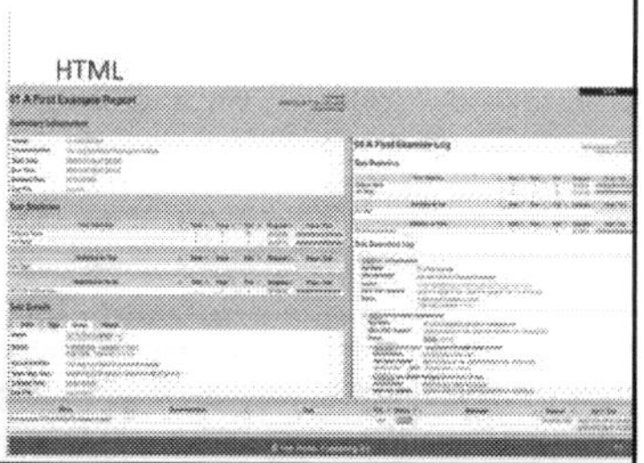

 95

CLI
MINGW64:/d/HiDrive/GitProjects/RobotFramework/robot-framework-workshop-master/answers
robfl@NitRobFl4 MINGW64 /d/HiDrive/GitProjects/RobotFramework/robot-framework-workshop-master
$ cd answers/
robfl@NitRobFl4 MINGW64 /d/HiDrive/GitProjects/RobotFramework/robot-framework-workshop-master/answers
$ ls -l
total 4
-rw-r--r-- 1 robfl 197609 331 okt 13 17:04 exercise_01.robot
-rw-r--r-- 1 robfl 197609 502 okt 13 17:04 exercise_02.robot
-rw-r--r-- 1 robfl 197609 496 okt 13 17:04 exercise_03.robot
-rw-r--r-- 1 robfl 197609 488 okt 13 17:04 exercise_04.robot
$ robot exercise_04.robot
Exercise 04 :: An example of using Robot Framework - Requests
Check that a valid HTTP call yields status 200 and the expected to... [WARN] Keyword 'RequestsLibrary.Ge
| PASS |
Exercise 04 :: An example of using Robot Framework - Requests | PASS |
1 critical test, 1 passed, 0 failed
1 test total, 1 passed, 0 failed
Output: D:\HiDrive\GitProjects\RobotFramework\robot-framework-workshop-master\answers\output.xml
Log: D:\HiDrive\GitProjects\RobotFramework\robot-framework-workshop-master\answers\log.html
Report: D:\HiDrive\GitProjects\RobotFramework\robot-framework-workshop-master\answers\report.html
© Van Haren Publishing BV.
96

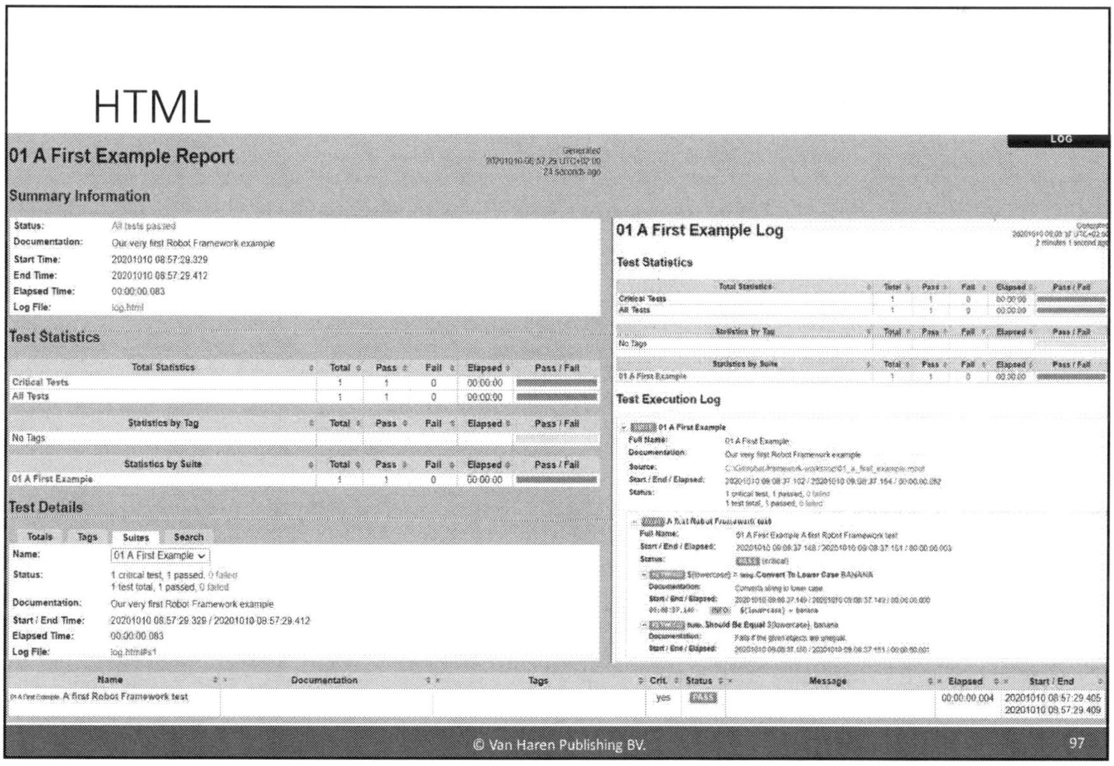
HTML
01 A First Example Report
Summary Information
Status: All tests passed
Documentation: Our very first Robot Framework example
Start Time: 20201010 08:57:29.329
End Time: 20201010 08:57:29.412
Elapsed Time: 00:00:00.083
Log File: log.html
Test Statistics
Test Details
01 A First Example Log
Test Execution Log
A first Robot Framework test
LOG
© Van Haren Publishing BV.
97

Visual Studio Code editor

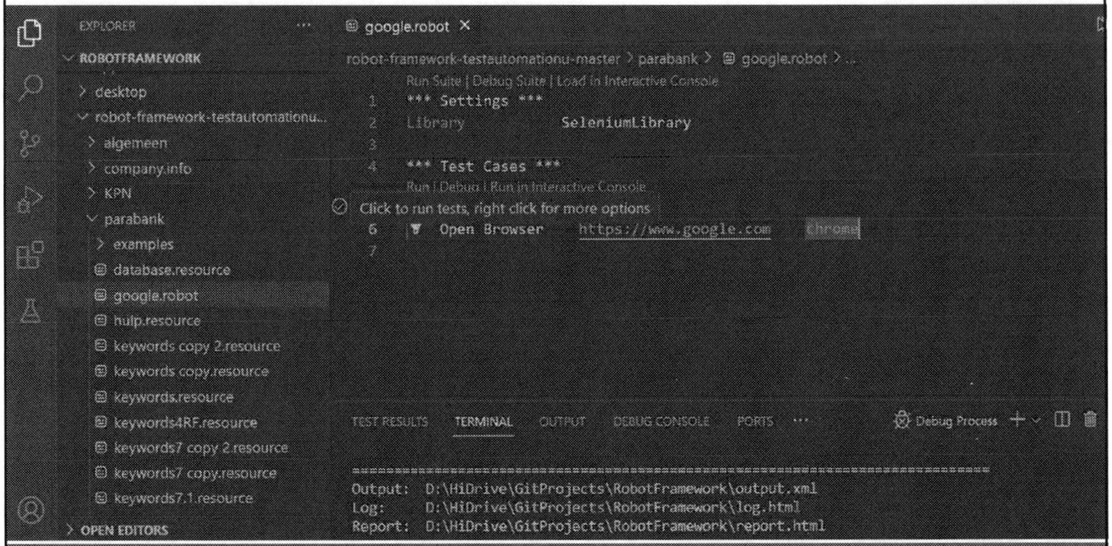

 98

The structure for ordering test cases

```
*** Settings ***
Documentation
Library

*** Variables ***
${MESSAGE}

*** Test Cases ***
My Test


Another Test

*** Keywords ***
My Keyword
```

Sections	To be used for
Settings	1) Importing test libraries, resource files and variable files 2) Defining metadata for test suites and test cases
Variables	Defining variables that can be used elsewhere in the test data
Test Cases	Creating test cases based on available keywords
Tasks	Creating tasks using available keywords.
Keywords	Creating user keywords based on existing keywords
Comments	Additional comments or information. Ignored by Robot Framework

 99

ROBOT FRAMEWORK/

 100

To work

ROBOT FRAMEWORK/

Exercise: *Visit the ParaBank website and check if you are on the homepage*

To do this exercise you need the following commands:

- Open Browser
- Page Should Contain

To be found in:
https://robotframework.org/SeleniumLibrary/SeleniumLibrary.html

url: http://localhost:8080/parabank/index.htm?ConnType=JDBC

 101

To work

ROBOT FRAMEWORK

Exercise: *Log in with username and password*

To do this exercise you need the following commands:

- Input Text
- Input Password
- Click Button

username: *john* and password: *demo*

Tip: Use F12 (right mouse button: Inspect (CTRL-shift-I) to select elements from the web page. Common term is "Dev Tools".

 102

To work

ROBOT FRAMEWORK

Exercise: *Open a new account*

To do this exercise you need the following commands:

- Click Link
- Select From List By ....

Open a new savings account number (SAVINGS) and check whether the new account exists and that there is an initial deposit.

Tip: In Dev Tools/Elements you can also find a link (href) and an id in addition to a class. You can also make a test on these elements.

 103

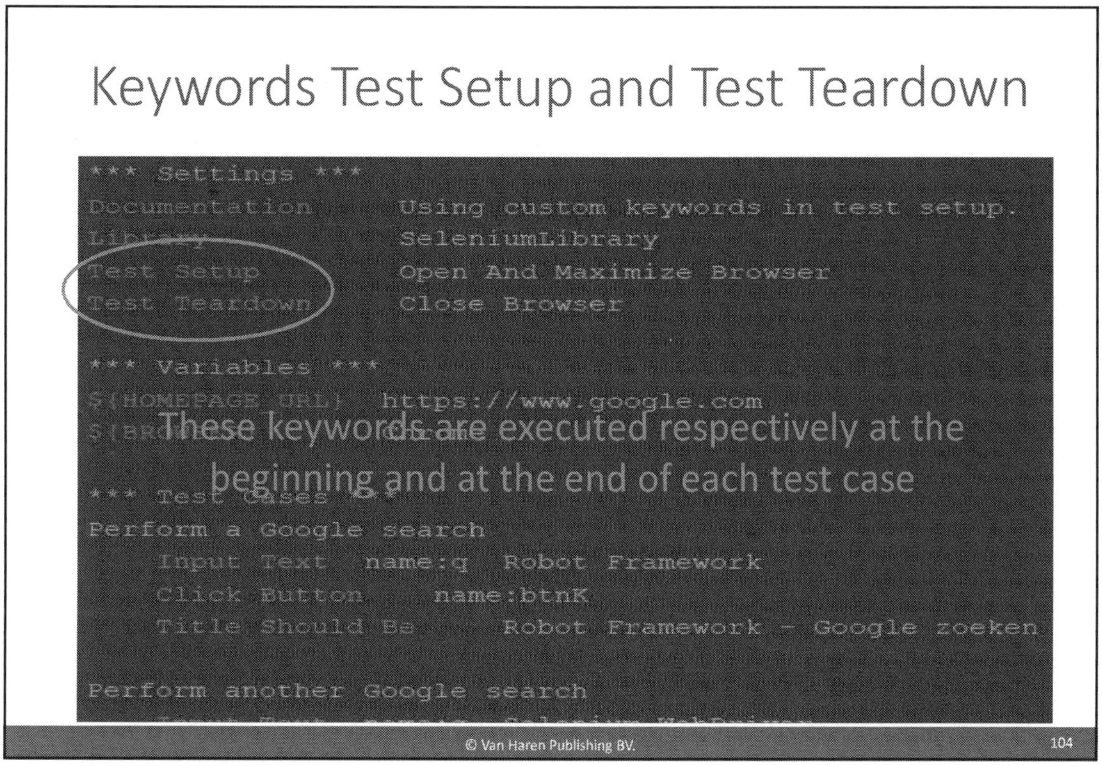
Keywords Test Setup and Test Teardown
*** Settings ***
Documentation   Using custom keywords in test setup.
Library   SeleniumLibrary
Test Setup   Open And Maximize Browser
Test Teardown   Close Browser
*** Variables ***
${HOMEPAGE URL}   https://www.google.com
These keywords are executed respectively at the beginning and at the end of each test case
*** Test Cases ***
Perform a Google search
Input Text   name:q   Robot Framework
Click Button   name:btnK
Title Should Be   Robot Framework - Google zoeken
Perform another Google search
© Van Haren Publishing BV.
104

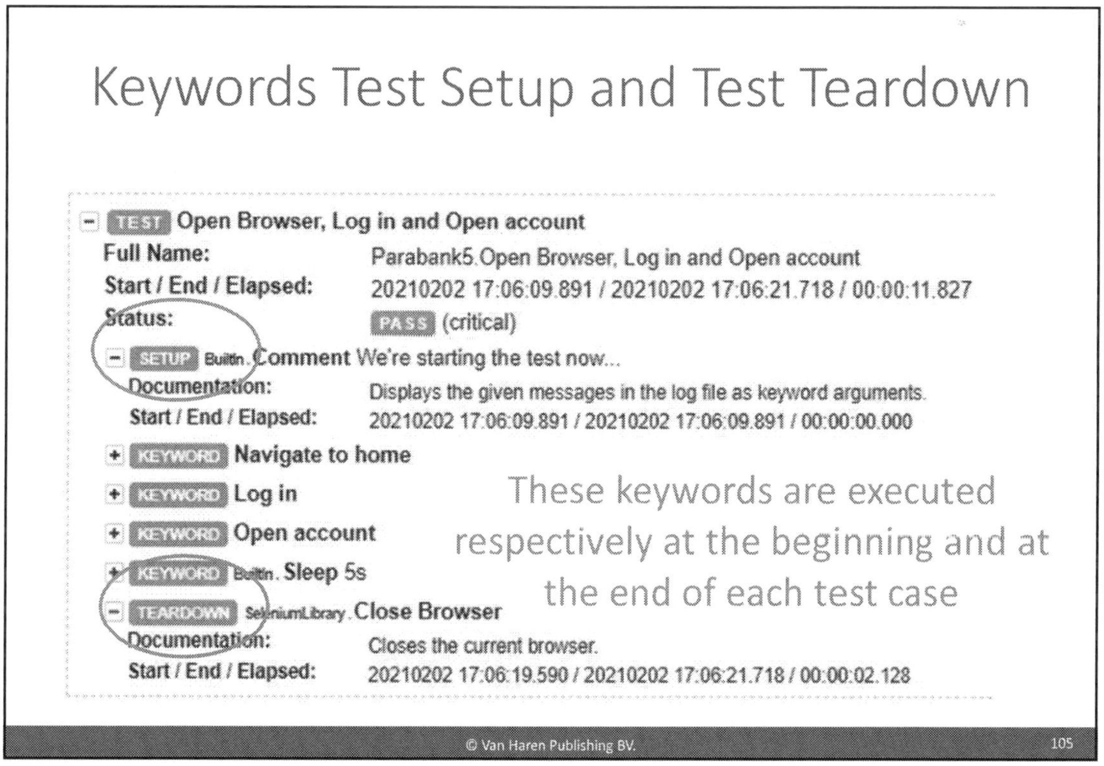
Keywords Test Setup and Test Teardown
TEST Open Browser, Log in and Open account
Full Name: Parabank5.Open Browser, Log in and Open account
Start / End / Elapsed: 20210202 17:06:09.891 / 20210202 17:06:21.718 / 00:00:11.827
Status: PASS (critical)
SETUP BuiltIn.Comment We're starting the test now...
Documentation: Displays the given messages in the log file as keyword arguments.
Start / End / Elapsed: 20210202 17:06:09.891 / 20210202 17:06:09.891 / 00:00:00.000
KEYWORD Navigate to home
KEYWORD Log in
KEYWORD Open account
KEYWORD BuiltIn.Sleep 5s
TEARDOWN SeleniumLibrary.Close Browser
Documentation: Closes the current browser.
Start / End / Elapsed: 20210202 17:06:19.590 / 20210202 17:06:21.718 / 00:00:02.128
These keywords are executed respectively at the beginning and at the end of each test case
© Van Haren Publishing BV.
105

To work

Exercise: Test Setup and Test Teardown

To do this exercise you need the following commands:

- Test Setup *"Open Browser"*
- Test Teardown *"Close Browser"*

Tip: Wait a few seconds to close the browser by using a "sleep" command

 106

Close Browser

At the end of the day, life should really be asking us:

Saving Changes?

 107

Program

- **Day 1**
- ~~Test tool overview~~
- ~~Working with:~~
  - ~~Selenium IDE~~
  - ~~Postman~~
  - Robot Framework

- **Day 2**
- Test roles
- Continuous testing
- Working with:
  - Robot Framework
  - Cypress
  - BrowserStack

 109

Test roles

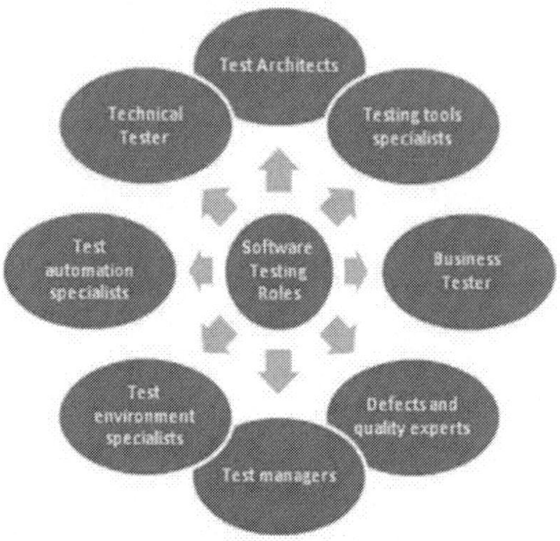

COU SEWARE

Who is responsible for creating automation code - developer or tester?

Do you let the testers automate their work?

Or do you let the developers automate the work?

Or is there another option?

 111

Who is responsible for creating automation code - developer or tester?

- Letting testers and developers automate both has pros and cons:
  - Testers know how to test, and
  - Developers are generally better at automation
- Whose time can be used for this?
  - A developer who spends time on test automation has less time for development
  - For a tester, it is deducted from the time he needs for the tests that are not (yet) automated
- And deadlines keep running

 112

Let developers develop, let testers test

A new role supporting the tester:
the automation engineer

 113

Automation engineers

- They do just that: support testing
- One-on-one automating of manual tests is virtually pointless
- Optimize testing and automate what runs repeatedly
- Keep clear why you do it and above all else:
  relate the time invested in it to the risk associated with it

 114

Will test automation replace manual testing?

Yes, if only to a certain extent.

Recurring tests are often easy to automate, through which you can check whether known problems do not occur (again) in a new version.

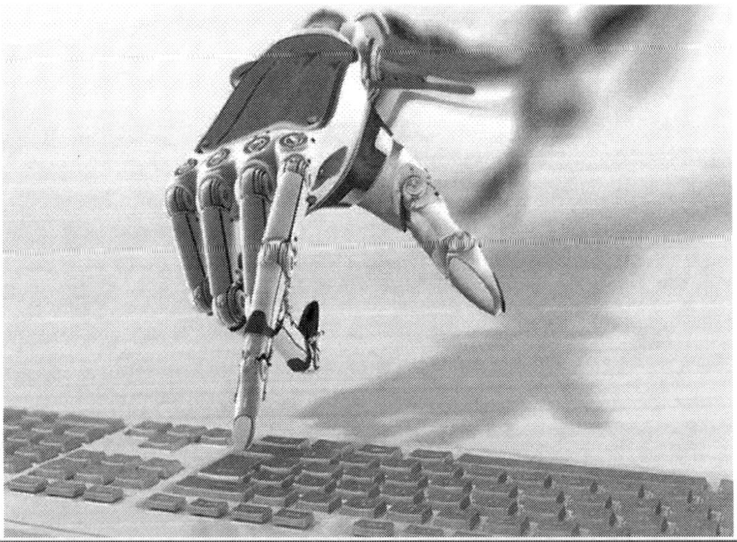

 115

Will automation replace manual testing?

- And do you automate the same tests you now perform manually?
  - **Yes and no**: not all manual tests are easy to automate but in some situations automation can do more than what a person could do during a manual test
  - It is therefore wise to think carefully about how you set up the automatic test, especially if you have many separate tests that have overlapping properties

 116

Do you find more errors with manual testing?

The main difference between manual testing and automatic testing is that manual testing does not necessarily detect more defects, but often *other defects*.

This is actually not that surprising, because in addition to the test case you are running, you also pay attention to other things.

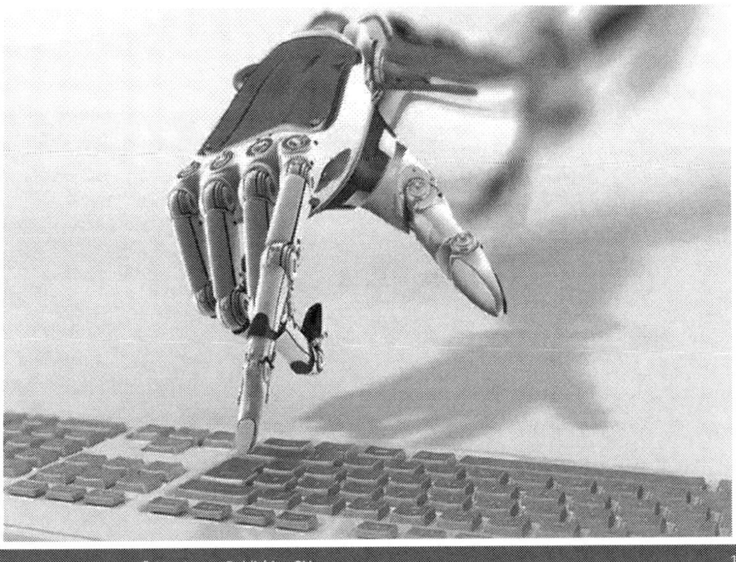

 117

What is a testing pyramid?

- Testing pyramid is a framework that can facilitate both developers and testers in building high-quality software
- The testing pyramid describes the test types that the development and QA teams should incorporate in an automated test suite

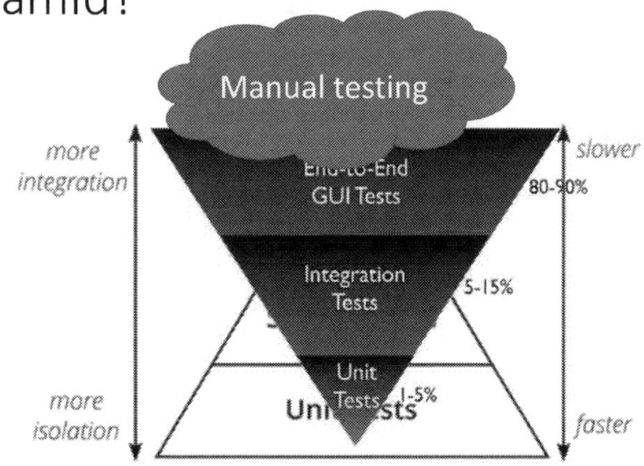

 118

Testing pyramid

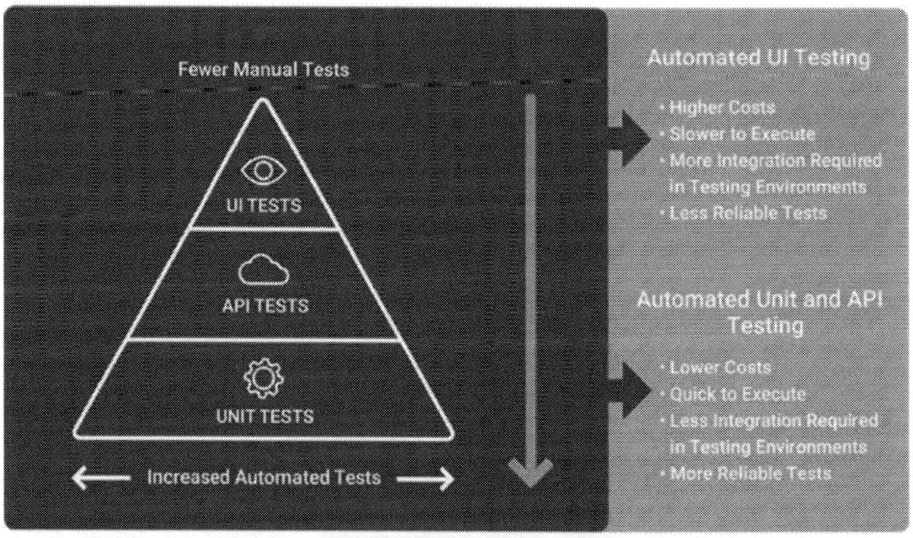

 119

Why automated testing lags

- In most cases the aim is to avoid the effort involved in transitioning from a manual test process to an automated test process
- We tend to reassure the organization that only adding UI test automation to their existing testing processes will suffice
- If there is no initiative from the Agile or DevOps teams, testers do not usually take the initiative in implementing changes

 120

Why automated testing lags

Most older testing tools and processes are unsuitable for the type of *Continuous Testing* that Agile and DevOps require because of:

- Inability to "shift left":
  - Testing can usually only be done late in each sprint when the UI and dependent components such as back-end APIs are finally completed and available for testing

- Slow execution time:
  - Tests are time consuming to run so it is not practical to run the complete regression test series on every build
  - This means the team has no direct feedback on whether their changes will impact the existing user experience

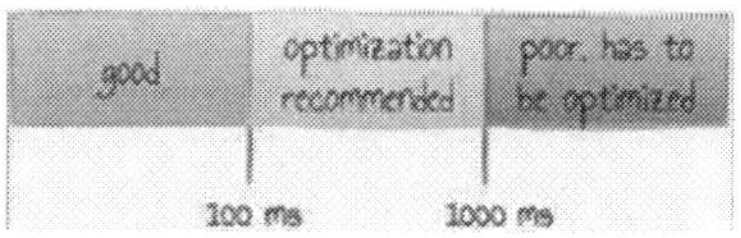

 121

Why automated testing lags

- The suggestion there is no more work after automating the tests is a myth:
  - Maintenance of the test design and test scripts will always be necessary!
  - Over time, as the testing becomes more robust, this may diminish
  - However, it still requires an upfront investment to get things right and ultimately enable potential cost savings, especially time savings, without quality loss

Personal note: *test automation is independent from the development methods used, it can be performed in waterfall, hybrid and Agile (DevOps) environments*

 122

Working with Robot Framework 2

COURSEWARE

Resource files

- *Resource files* are imported using the Resource setting in Settings

```
*** Settings ***
Documentation     An example resource file
Library           SeleniumLibrary
Resource          ${RESOURCES}/common.resource
```

- When creating resource files, it is possible to use the normal .robot extension, but the special .resource extension is recommended to separate resource files from test case files especially when you are running through CI/CD pipelines

Resource file structure

- The structure of resource files is the same as that of test case files
- The variables and keywords are used in exactly the same way as in test case files

```
*** Keywords ***
Navigate to home
    Open Browser    ${SiteUrl}    ${Browser}
    Maximize Browser Window
    Log Title
    Page Should Contain    ${text}
```

Back to work

Exercise: Resource files

So far you have included all test data, sections, keywords and variables in your test script.

The task now is to modify the test script in such a way that *keywords* end up in a separate resource file.

To do this exercise you need the following commands:

- Resource *filename*.resource
- *** Keywords ***

 126

Variables

- All test data files can import variables with the Variables setting

```
*** Variables ***
${VARIABLE}             An example string
${ANOTHER VARIABLE}     This is pretty easy!
${INTEGER}              ${42}
@{STRINGS}              one          two           kolme        four
@{NUMBERS}              ${1}         ${INTEGER}    ${3.14}
&{MAPPING}              one=${1}     two=${2}      three=${3}
@{ANIMALS}              cat          dog
&{FINNISH}              cat=kissa    dog=koira
```

- All variables from a variable file are available in the test data file it imports
- If multiple variable files have been imported and they contain a variable with the same name, the variable in the earliest imported file will be taken

 127

To work

Exercise: Variables

So far you have hard coded all variable data into your test script.

Create a separate section in which the variables from the test script are grouped.

To do this exercise you need the following commands:

- Resource   variables.resource
- *** Variables ***

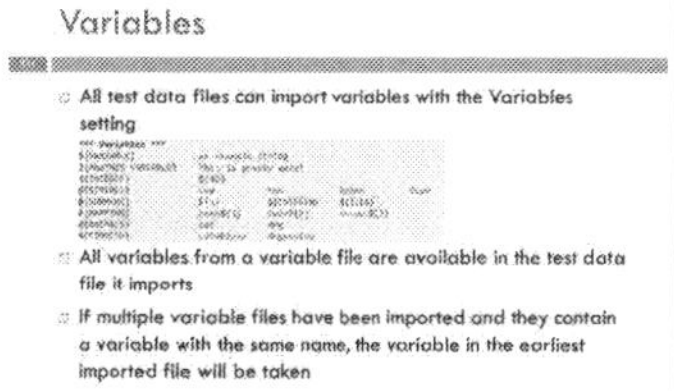
Variables

- All test data files can import variables with the Variables setting
- All variables from a variable file are available in the test data file it imports
- If multiple variable files have been imported and they contain a variable with the same name, the variable in the earliest imported file will be taken

 128

Page Object Model (POM)

- Page Object Model, also known as POM, is a design pattern in Selenium that creates an object repository for storing all web elements
- It helps reduce code duplication and improves test case maintenance
- In Page Object Model, consider each web page of an application as a class file
- A page object represents a part of your web application
  - An e-commerce web application might have a home page, a listings page and a checkout page. Each of them can be represented by page object models.

COURSEWARE

ROBOT FRAMEWORK/ Web services

- You'll think there are quite a few Rest API testing frameworks out there already, such as Postman, SoapUI, SOATest, and Rest-Assured
- Another one on the list is Robot Framework

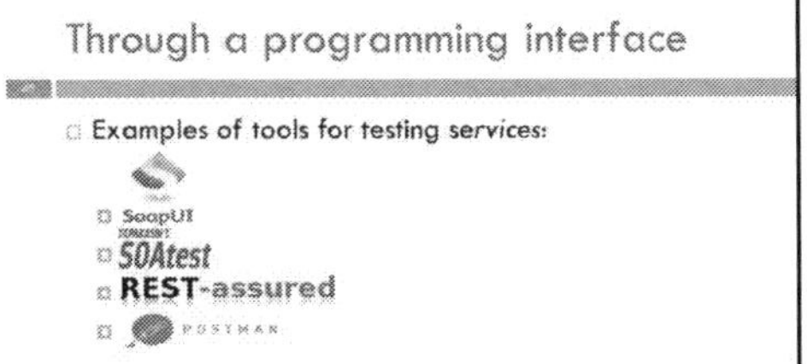

 130

 131

To work

Exercise: Get request

The first task is a so-called Get request on John Smith's "Accounts overview".

To make sure that the assignment was successful, you can request the status code '200'.

To do this exercise you need the following commands:

- Library RequestsLibrary
- GET On Session (Get Request depricated)
- Status Should Be

 132

To work

Exercise: Post request

Open New Account or Transfer money from one account to a contra account and check whether the transferred money is in the contra account. Or Request for a loan.

To do this exercise you need the following commands:

- POST On Session (POST Request depricated)
- Status Should Be
- GET On Session (Get Request depricated)

 133

ROBOT FRAMEWORK/

Robot Framework

- Robot Framework has a vibrant community around it with various online forums, an annual RoboCon conference, and meetup groups around the world
- https://robotframework.org/
- https://testautomationu.applitools.com/robot-framework-tutorial/
- great examples and online documentation on GitHub

 134

Working with Cypress

COURSEWARE

Tool selection

cucumber

ROBOT FRAMEWORK

cypress
Test your code, not your patience

 136

cypress

- Cypress is an open source testing tool
  - Being open source means that Cypress is *basically* free to use with no license fees
- Cypress was founded in 2014 with a mission to build a thriving, open source ecosystem that increases productivity, makes testing an enjoyable experience and generates developer happiness
- Cypress simplifies test setup, writing, executing and debugging

 137

cypress

- Cypress is not necessarily better but different
- Why different?
  - Built by frontend developers
  - For frontend developers
- "Javascript only" because frontend developers program in Javascript

 138

cypress

- Cypress was built for frontend developers, but that doesn't mean testers can't take advantage!
- Whatever framework the application or website is built in (*React*, *Angular*, *Vue*), it can be tested with Javascript, as long as it runs in a web browser
- With Cypress you can write all kinds of tests:
  - Unit tests
  - Integration tests
  - End-to-end tests
- It contains known unit test tools like *Mocha*, *Chai*, *Sinon* and *Jest*
- And because all these tools are already available, you can focus on what is really important: writing tests

 139

cypress

- A very important difference between Cypress and Selenium is the way in which the interaction with the browser is set up:
  - Selenium communicates with the browser via HTTP, making it subject to possible delays
  - Cypress has its own mechanism to manipulate the browser and the browser works directly in the GUI of Cypress, without network communication, meaning that Cypress works significantly faster and is less prone to hiccups

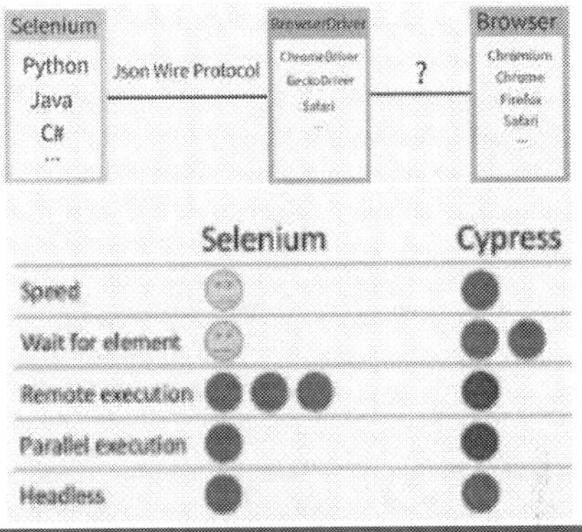

 140

What makes Cypress different?

- Time travel:
  - Cypress takes snapshots while the tests are running
  - Hover over commands to see exactly what happened at each step
- Debuggability:
  - Debug directly from well-known tools like Chrome DevTools
  - The errors and stack traces make debugging lightning fast
- Real time reloads:
  - Cypress automatically reloads when you make changes to your tests
  - See the commands executed in real time in the app
- Automatic waiting:
  - Cypress waits for commands and assertions before proceeding

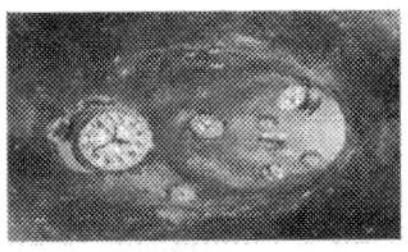

 141

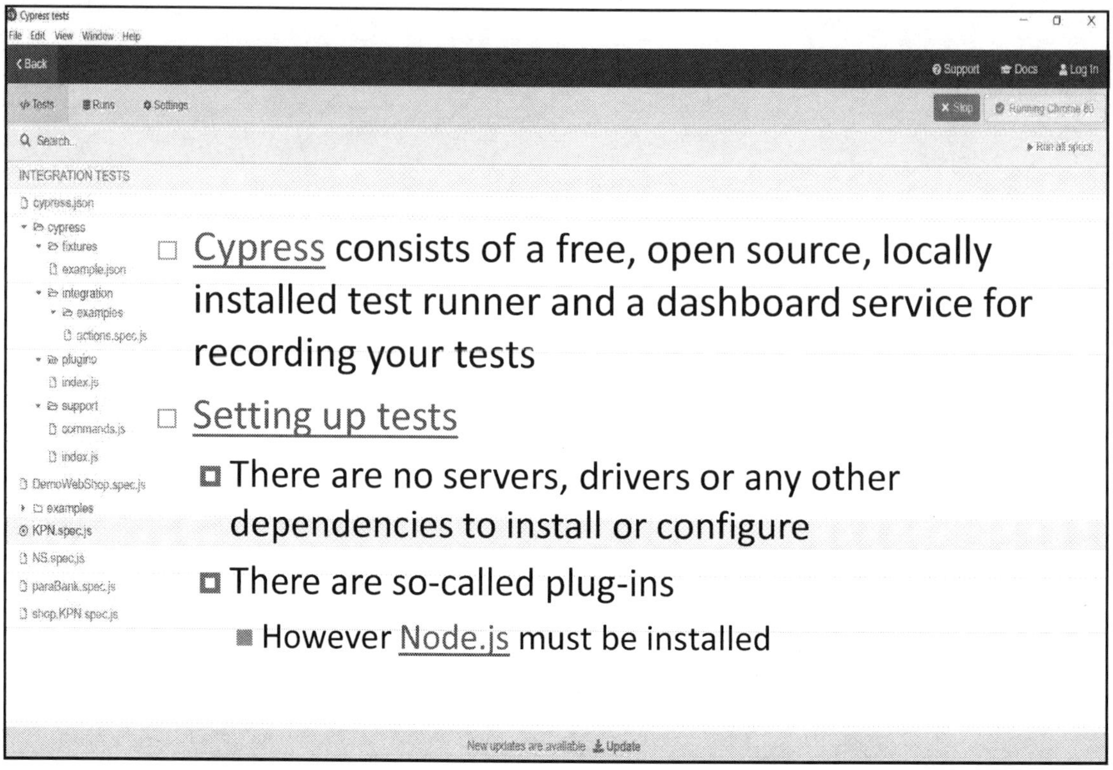
Cypress consists of a free, open source, locally installed test runner and a dashboard service for recording your tests
Setting up tests
There are no servers, drivers or any other dependencies to install or configure
There are so-called plug-ins
However Node.js must be installed

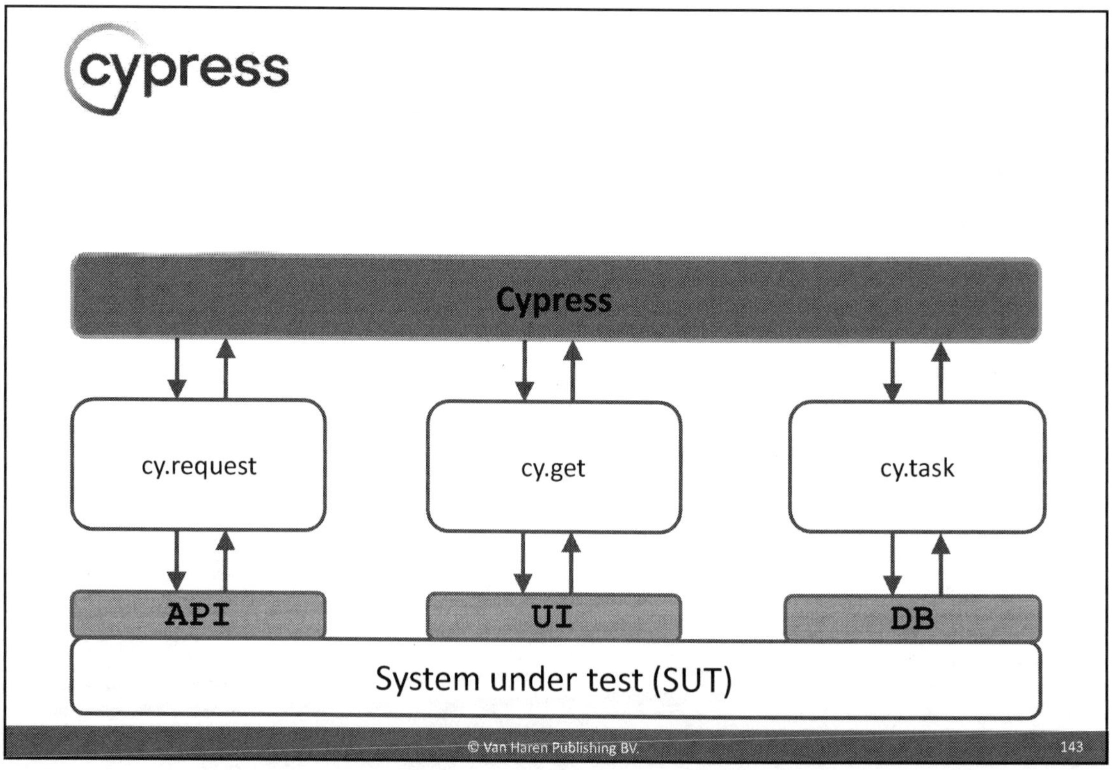
cypress
Cypress
cy.request
cy.get
cy.task
API
UI
DB
System under test (SUT)
© Van Haren Publishing BV.
143

The Document Object Model (DOM)

- The Document Object Model (DOM) is a cross-platform and language-independent interface that treats an HTML or XML document as a tree structure wherein each node is an object representing a part of the document
- The DOM represents a document with a logical tree
  - Each branch of the tree ends in a node, and each node contains objects.

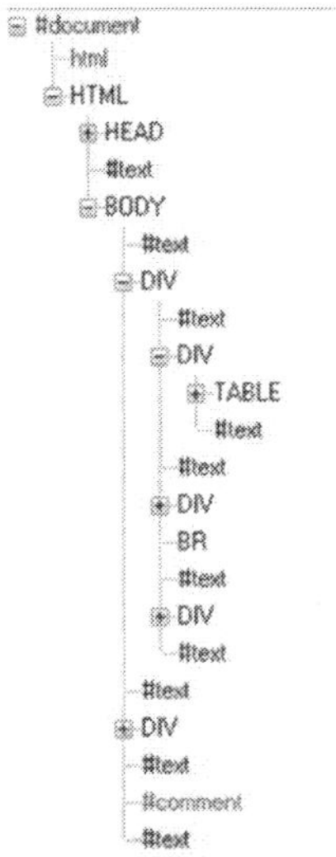

https://en.wikipedia.org/wiki/Document_Object_Model

Setting up Cypress

Required:

- NodeJS
- NPM = NodeJS Package Manager
  - Like Maven for JAVA
- Cypress via: *npm install cypress*
  - Start Cypress*: npx cypress open*

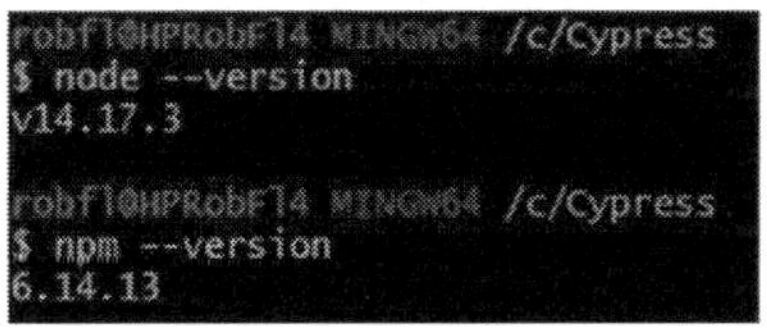

 145

Setting up Cypress

Visual Studio Code
App

Code editors:

- Visual Studio Code
- Atom, Eclipse, IntelliJ IDEA, and WebStorm are the most popular alternatives and competitors to Visual Studio Code

PyCharm

Visual Studio

Sublime Text is available for OS X, Windows and Linux.

 146

Cypress test runner

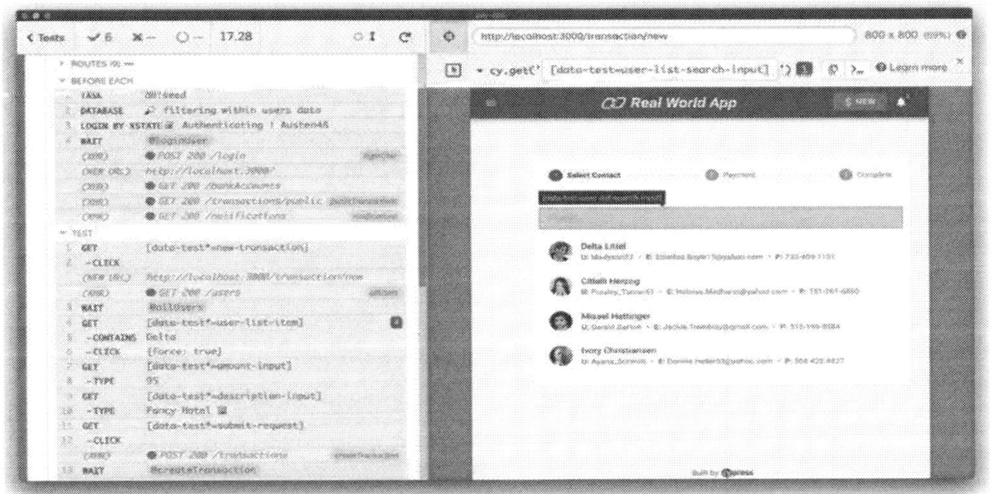

Command Log

App preview

 147

 148

To work

Exercise:

Again, visit the ParaBank webpage and check if you are on the homepage

To do this exercise you need the following commands:

- cy.visit()
- cy.title()

Documentation:

- https://docs.cypress.io/api/commands/visit
- https://docs.cypress.io/api/commands/title

url: http://localhost:8080/parabank/
https://parabank.parasoft.com/parabank/

 149

To work

Exercise

Log-in with username and password

To do this exercise you need the following commands:

- cy.get()
  - type() username: *john*
  - type() password: *demo*
- cy.click()

Tip: Use F12 (right mouse button: Inspect (CTRL-shift-I) to select elements from the web page

Commonly used term is "Dev Tools".

To work

Exercise:

Open a new account

To do this exercise you need the following commands:

- cy.get()
- select()
- should()

Open a new savings account number (SAVINGS) and check whether the new account exists and that there is a first deposit.

Tip: in Dev Tools / Elements you can find a link (href) as well as an id in addition to a class. You can also make a test on these elements.

What is continuous testing?

Continuous testing is the process of running automated tests as part of the software delivery pipeline in order to get feedback on the business risks of a delivery as quickly as possible

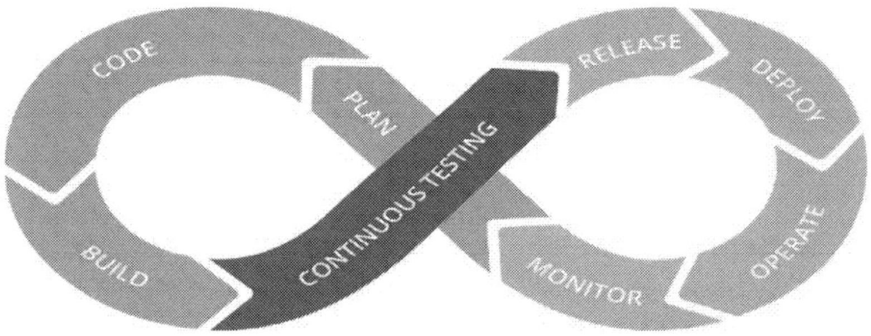

 152

Continuous testing

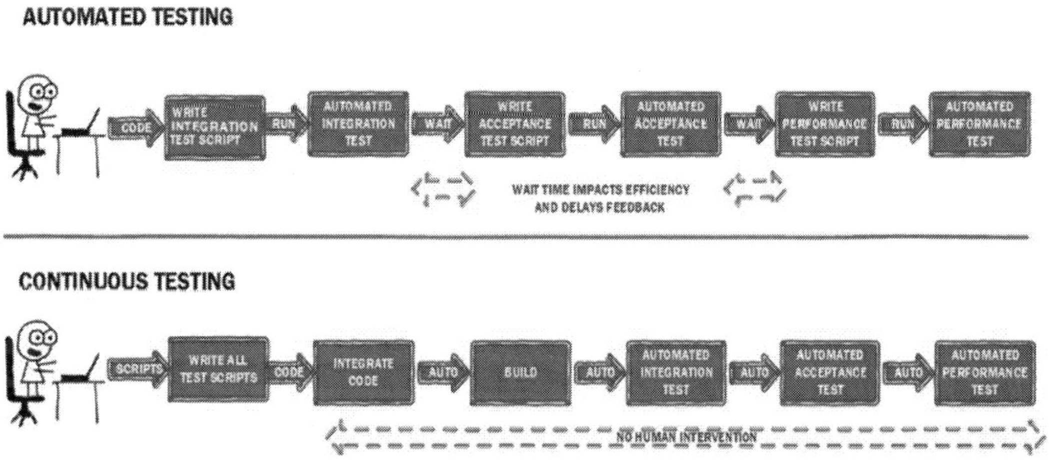

COURSEWARE

Continuous testing

- Continuous testing provides immediate insight into whether a release candidate is too risky to go through the software delivery pipeline
- Continuous testing expects testing to be embedded in the development process, not addressed at the end
- It is seamlessly integrated into the software delivery pipeline and DevOps-toolchain

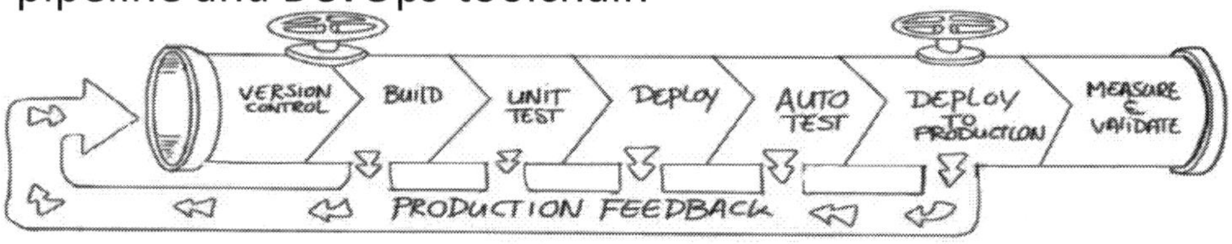

 154

Continuous testing

- Everyone understands that Agile and DevOps are all about change
- It is transforming people, processes and technologies to deliver innovative software as quickly as possible
- Despite all these changes, one thing seems to remain the same: the software testing process

 155

Continuous testing

- The software testing process:
  - A recent study reports that 80% of organizations have adopted Agile, but only 20% have automated testing
  - In other words, test processes have persisted in the past, even if organizations have invested a lot of time and effort in transforming their development processes to meet the business demands of today and tomorrow

 156

Deployment pipeline

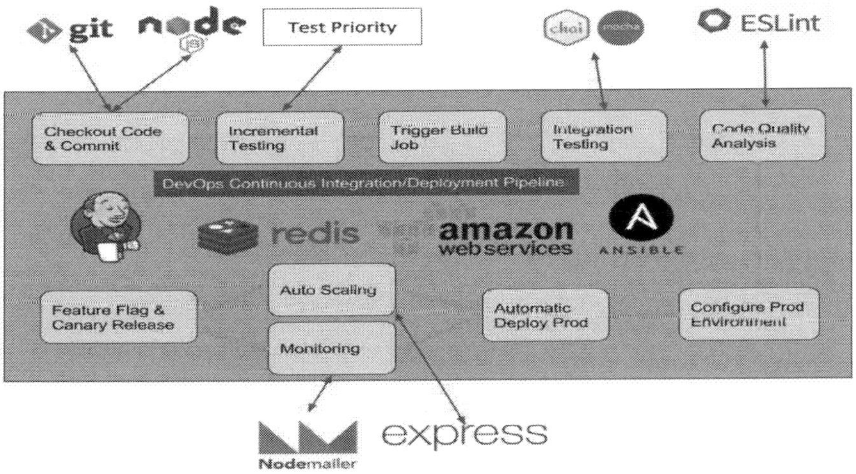

 157

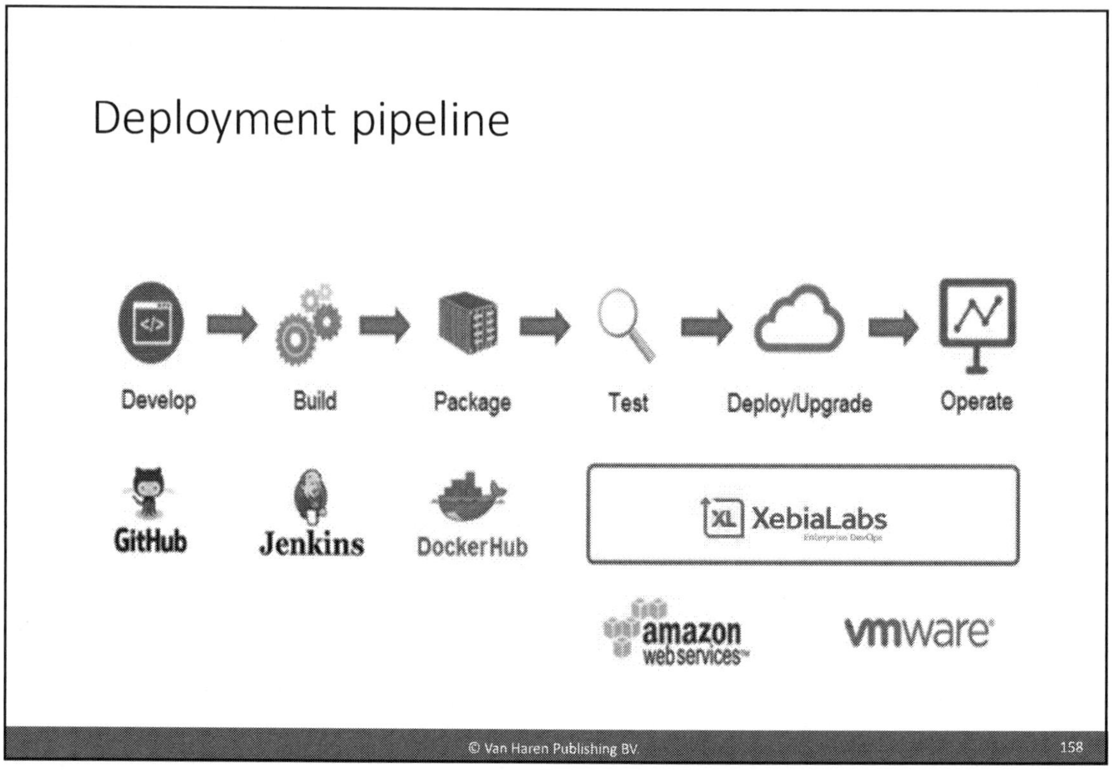

git GitHub GitLab

- Git is an open source version control system
- Each Git project contains the full repository with a complete historical overview and full tracking capabilities
- GitHub & GitLab are popular hosting platforms that offer both free and private repositories

 159

Jenkins <> GitLab

- Jenkins and GitLab are open source automation servers
- Can help to automate the parts of software development related to building, testing and deploying, thus facilitating continuous integration and continuous delivery
- Builds can be triggered in several ways, for example by committing in a version control system, by scheduling through a cron-like mechanism, and by requesting a specific build URL

 161

Pipeline

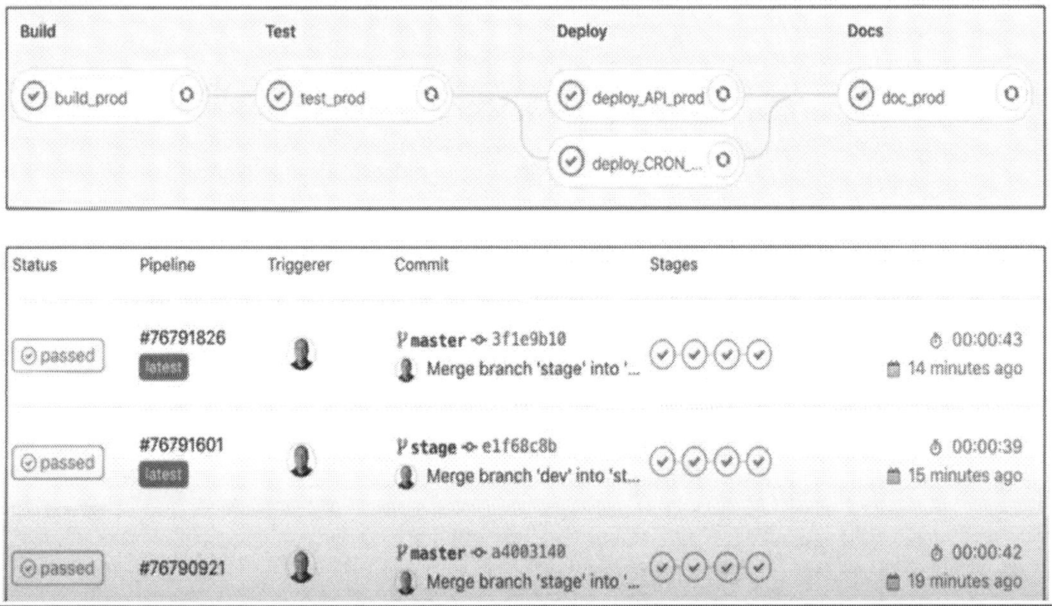

 162

Jenkins & GitLab

- GitLab is integrated with GitLab Software Configuration Management (SCM) as pipelines can be created using GitLab
- Whereas Jenkins is considered to be the best build tool in the software industry
- Jenkins is an open-source continuous integration server that is extendable with plug-ins

 163

Jenkins & GitLab

- Jenkins/Gitlab sends emails to the specified recipients when a certain important event occurs, such as:
  - Failed build
  - Unstable build
  - Successful build after a failed build, indicating that a crisis is over
  - Unstable build after a successful one, indicating that there's a regression

 164

Of course it is not all fun and games

- For example, tests can only be written in *JavaScript*
  - No problem of course for frontend developers, but it may be a reason to choose a different framework for others
- '*Flakiness*': No async hell, despite Cypress neatly waiting for the state you want, until the testing continues

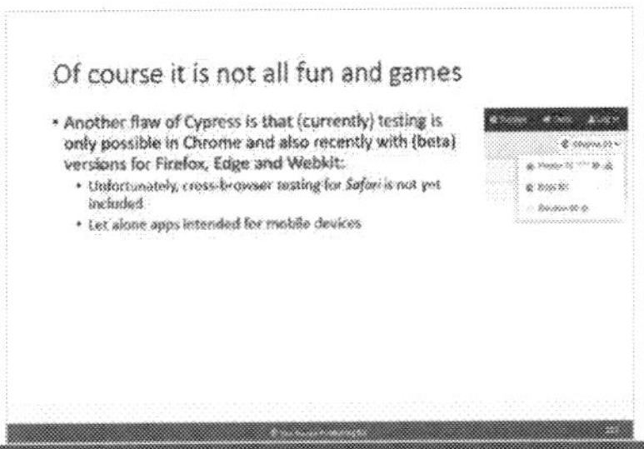

© Van Haren Publishing BV. 166

Of course it is not all fun and games

- Another flaw of Cypress is that (currently) testing is only possible in Chrome and also recently with (beta) versions for Firefox, Edge and Webkit:
  - Unfortunately, cross-browser testing for *Safari* is not yet included
  - Let alone apps intended for mobile devices

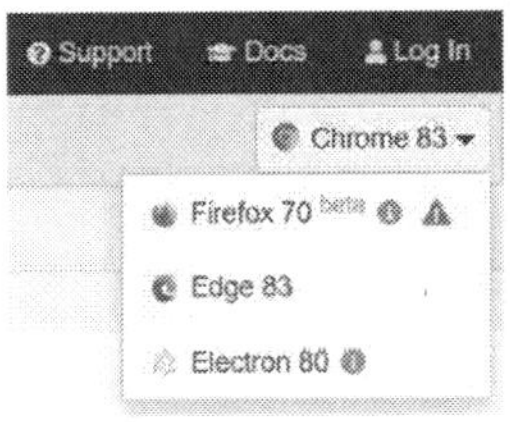

© Van Haren Publishing BV. 167

Working with BrowserStack

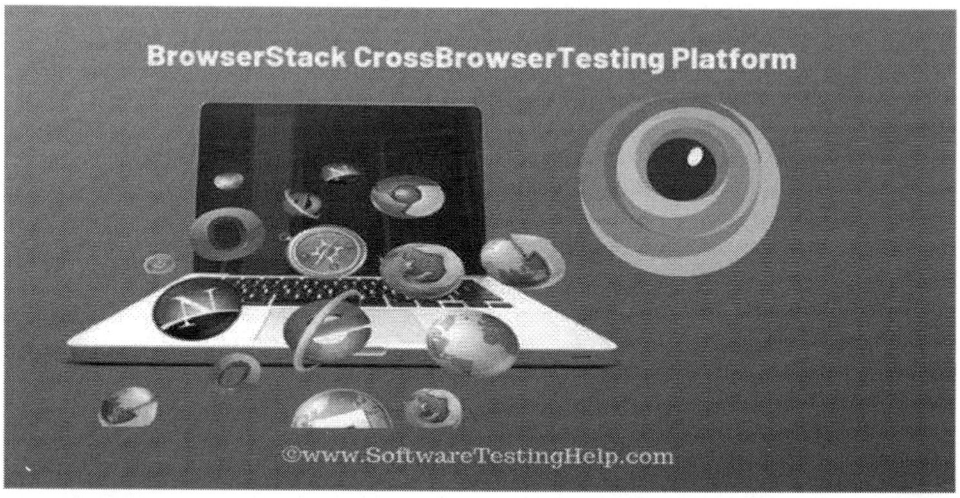

It's all about browsers and devices

- With popular browsers such as *Chrome* and *Safari* now available, you could almost forget that for a long time Internet Explorer was the only gateway to the internet for many consumers
- Optimization was also considerably easier: support Internet Explorer and your website works optimally for almost all visitors
- But times change!

Support visitors instead of browsers

- Nowadays there is a seperate app for every need
- And we have access to the internet not only on PCs, but also via *smartphones* and *tablets,* with different screen sizes, different operating systems and a choice of browsers

 170

Support visitors instead of browsers

- This creates new challenges, not just for developers and web designers, but importantly also for testers
- In order to optimally meet the wishes of the client, it is important to agree in advance which operating systems and browsers are to be supported

 171

Force users to update browsers

- Support for all devices, browsers and systems is, in most cases, simply not profitable, so it is important to make choices:
  - *Are we going to test on the latest devices from popular brands, such as the new iPhone that will be released soon?*
  - *Will we now only test newly developed apps, websites and platforms on iOS12 or also still on iOS6? And testing on the Samsung Galaxy S23 is obvious*

But how do we deal with the older Galaxy S6?

 172

BrowserStack

Do not cut corners on tablets and mobile phones

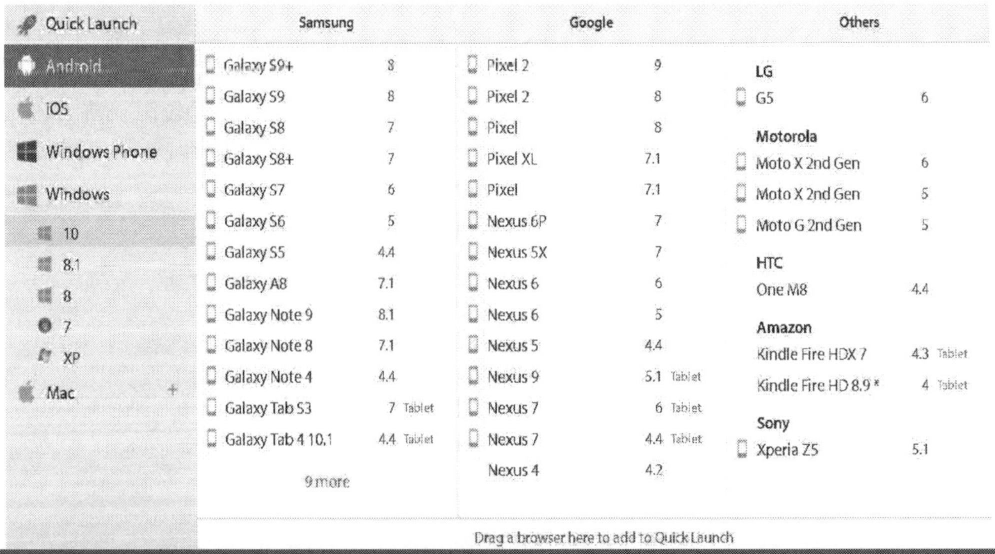

 173

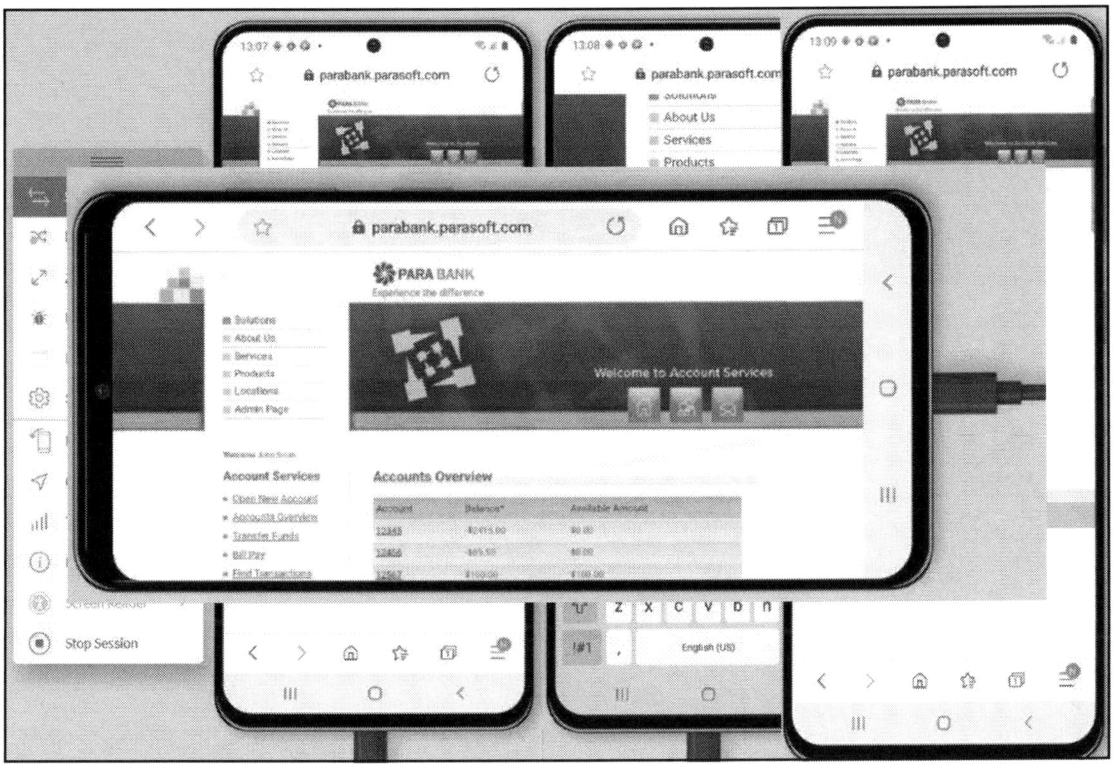
parabank.parasoft.com
PARA BANK
Welcome to Account Services
Account Services
Accounts Overview
About Us
Services
Products
Stop Session
English (US)

Quick Launch
Android
iOS
Windows
Mac
Big Sur
Catalina
Mojave
High Sierra
Sierra
El Capitan
Yosemite
Mavericks
Mountain Lion
Lion
Snow Leopard
Real Devices (55)
iPhone
iPad
iPhone 12 14
iPhone 12 Mini 14
iPhone 12 Pro Max 14
iPhone 11 Pro 13
iPhone 11 13
iPhone 11 14
iPhone 11 Pro Max 14
iPhone 11 Pro Max 13
iPhone 8 13
iPhone XS 14
iPhone XS 13
iPhone XS 12
iPhone XS Max 12
iPhone XR 12
iPhone 8 12
iPhone 7 12
iPhone 6S 12
iPhone X 11
iPhone 8 Plus 12
iPhone 8 Plus 11
iPhone 8 11
iPhone SE 2020 13
iPhone SE 11
iPhone 6S Plus 11
iPhone 6S 11
iPhone 6 11
iPhone 7 10
iPhone 6S Plus 9
iPhone 6S 9
iPhone 6 Plus 8
iPhone 6 8
iPhone 5S 7
Show 6 Simulators
Drag a browser here to add to Quick Launch
© Van Haren Publishing BV.
175

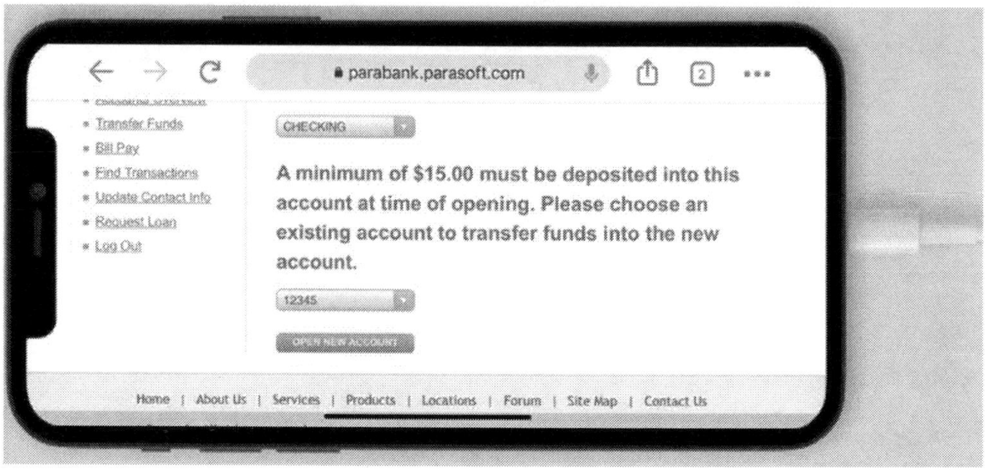
parabank.parasoft.com
Transfer Funds
Bill Pay
Find Transactions
Update Contact Info
Request Loan
Log Out
CHECKING
A minimum of $15.00 must be deposited into this account at time of opening. Please choose an existing account to transfer funds into the new account.
12345
OPEN NEW ACCOUNT
Home | About Us | Services | Products | Locations | Forum | Site Map | Contact Us

 176

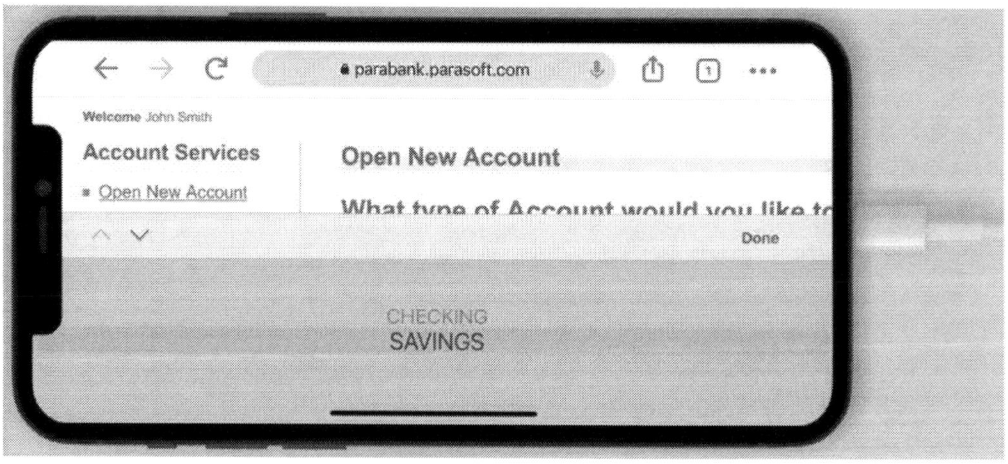
parabank.parasoft.com
Welcome John Smith
Account Services
Open New Account
Open New Account
What type of Account would you like
Done
CHECKING
SAVINGS

 177

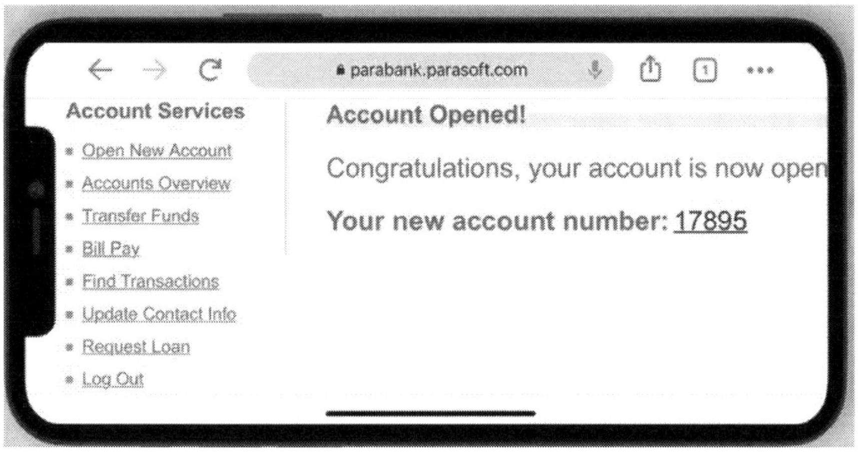
parabank.parasoft.com
Account Services
Open New Account
Accounts Overview
Transfer Funds
Bill Pay
Find Transactions
Update Contact Info
Request Loan
Log Out
Account Opened!
Congratulations, your account is now open
Your new account number: 17895

 178

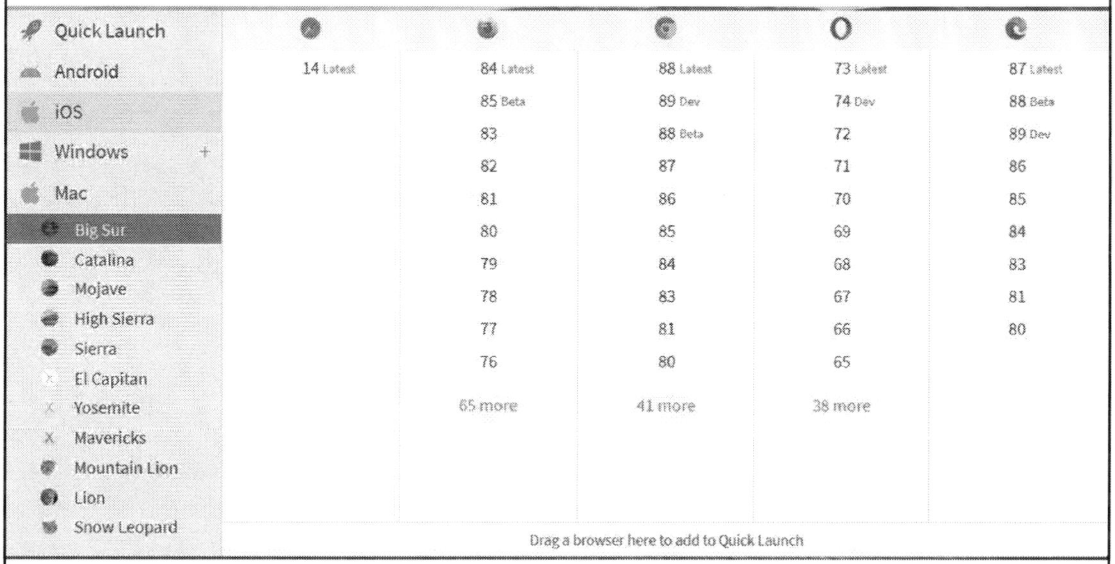
Quick Launch
Android
iOS
Windows
Mac
Big Sur
Catalina
Mojave
High Sierra
Sierra
El Capitan
Yosemite
Mavericks
Mountain Lion
Lion
Snow Leopard
14 Latest
84 Latest
85 Beta
83
82
81
80
79
78
77
76
65 more
88 Latest
89 Dev
88 Beta
87
86
85
84
83
81
80
41 more
73 Latest
74 Dev
72
71
70
69
68
67
66
65
38 more
87 Latest
88 Beta
89 Dev
86
85
84
83
81
80
Drag a browser here to add to Quick Launch

 179

Starting real Safari 14 on macOS Big Sur
Setting up a secure connection
Cancel
© Van Haren Publishing BV
180

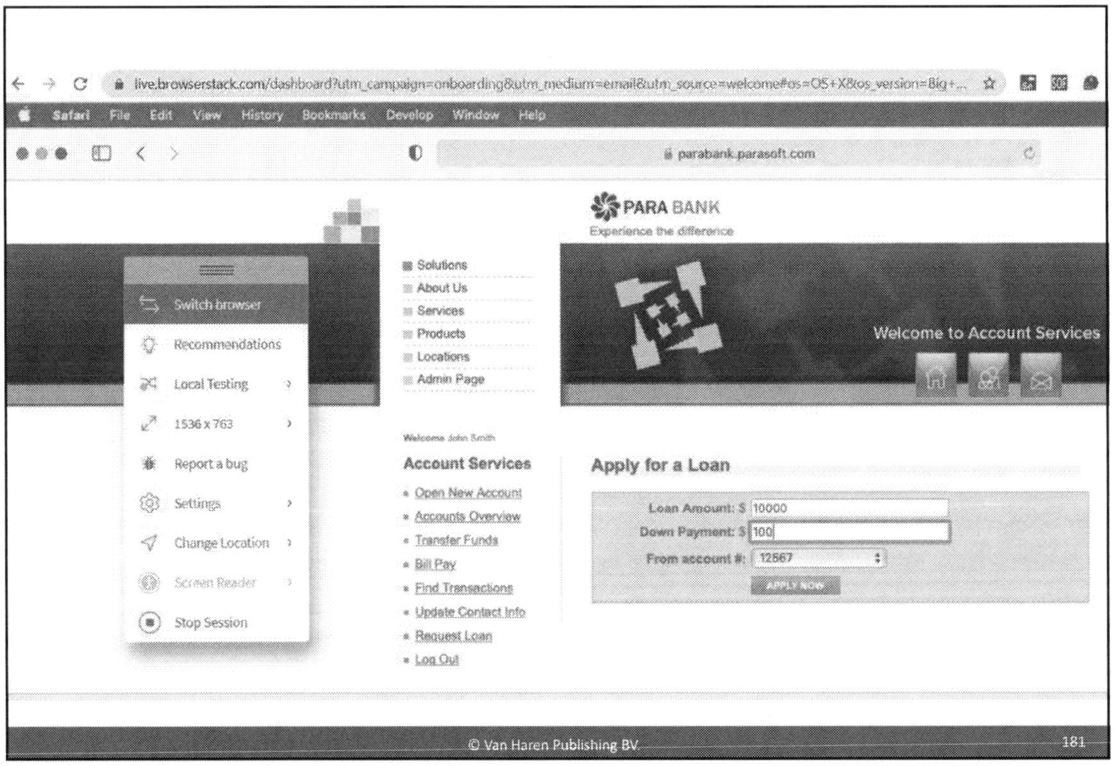
live.browserstack.com/dashboard?utm_campaign=onboarding&utm_medium=email&utm_source=welcome#os=OS+X&os_version=Big+...
Safari File Edit View History Bookmarks Develop Window Help
parabank.parasoft.com
PARA BANK
Experience the difference
Switch browser
Recommendations
Local Testing
1536 x 763
Report a bug
Settings
Change Location
Screen Reader
Stop Session
Solutions
About Us
Services
Products
Locations
Admin Page
Welcome to Account Services
Account Services
Open New Account
Accounts Overview
Transfer Funds
Bill Pay
Find Transactions
Update Contact Info
Request Loan
Log Out
Apply for a Loan
Loan Amount: $ 10000
Down Payment: $ 100
From account #: 12567
APPLY NOW
© Van Haren Publishing BV
181

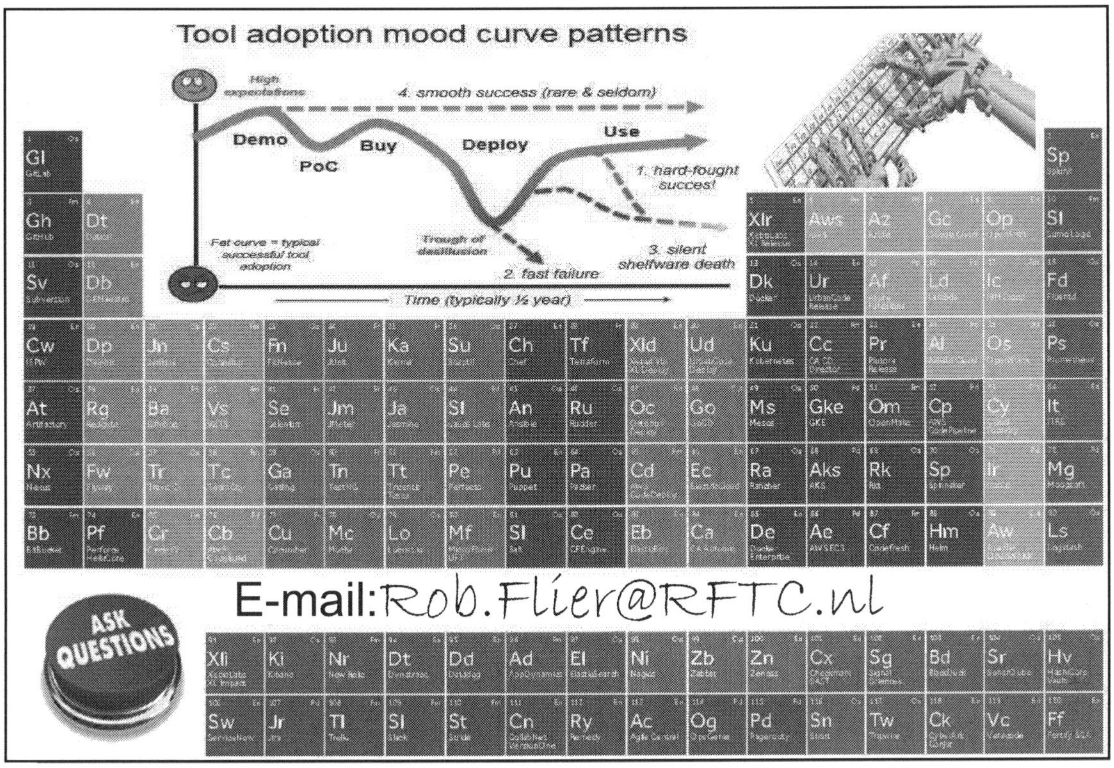
Tool adoption mood curve patterns
High expectations
4. smooth success (rare & seldom)
Demo
PoC
Buy
Deploy
Use
1. hard-fought succes!
Trough of desillusion
Fat curve = typical successful tool adoption
2. fast failure
3. silent shelfware death
Time (typically ½ year)
ASK QUESTIONS
E-mail:Rob.Flier@RFTC.nl

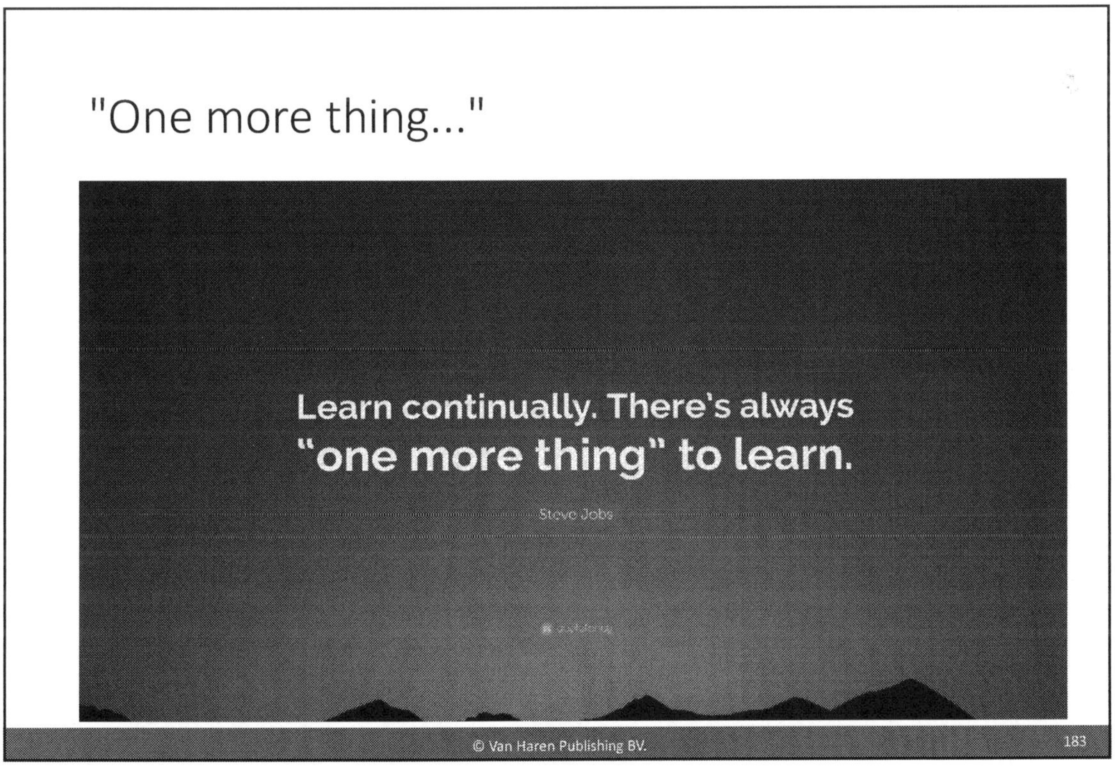
"One more thing..."
Learn continually. There's always
"one more thing" to learn.
Steve Jobs
© Van Haren Publishing BV.
183

 184

ASSIGNMENTS ROBOTFRAMEWORK & CYPRESS

Assignments Robotframework & Cypress

A training without assignments is like a ship model in a box. The model looks beautiful on the box in the store.

You can take the package home with you, but as long as you don't take the time to assemble the package, it will never be a three-master.

So I would like you to practise what you have learned during the training. The assignments below will help you with this.

First, I will give you a number of tips that increase the chance that your assignment can actually be carried out. Then I also give you background information about the importance of assignments. And of course the elaboration of the assignment is not lacking.

After completing these assignments, you will have developed a basis for further developing the test by testing other functions.

Good luck with the assignments!

Rob Flier

Content

Robot Framework for GUI's (websites)

Exercise robot-1: Visit the webpage and check if you are on the homepage

To do this exercise you need the following commands:

- Open Browser (https://robotframework.org/SeleniumLibrary/SeleniumLibrary.html#Open%20Browser)
- Page Should Contain (https://robotframework.org/SeleniumLibrary/SeleniumLibrary.html#Page%20Should%20Contain)

To be found in: https://robotframework.org/SeleniumLibrary/SeleniumLibrary.html
url: http://localhost:8080/parabank of https://parabank.parasoft.com/parabank/index.htm

In your project folder you have a folder called "parabank". In this folder create a new test file "parabank.robot" and copy the code below:

```
*** Settings ***
Library  SeleniumLibrary

*** Test Cases ***
Testcase My First RobotFramework Test Case
```

1. Now write your test and save the test.

2. You can start the test in Visual Studio Code or in a CLI, e.g. command.exe, Git bash.

   The command to execute: *robot parabank.robot*
   Destination folder: c:\robotTest/parabank

   In Git bash cd ../../RobotTest/parabank

3. After the test has run you can in the browser via command:
   C:\Robot\parabank\report.html

Tip! Install the following extension: **Robot Framework Language Server** from the Extensions menu item to the left of the screen.
With this plug in you can run your test scripts by clicj=king on the Run button.

Exercise robot-2: Log in with username and password

To do this exercise you need the following commands:

- Input Text (https://robotframework.org/SeleniumLibrary/SeleniumLibrary.html#Input%20Text)
- Input Password (https://robotframework.org/SeleniumLibrary/SeleniumLibrary.html#Input%20Password)
- Click Button (https://robotframework.org/SeleniumLibrary/SeleniumLibrary.html#Click%20Button)

Username= *john*
Password: *demo*

Tip: Use F12 (right mouse button: Inspect (CTRL-shift-I) to select elements from the web page. Common term is "Dev Tools".

Exercise robot-3: Open a new account

To do this exercise you need the following commands:

- Click Link
- Select From List By ....
- Click Element

Open a new savings account (SAVINGS) and check whether the new account exists and that there is an initial deposit.

Tip: in Dev Tools / Elements you can find a link (href) as well as an id in addition to a class. You can also make a test on these elements.

Exercise robot-4: Test setup and Test teardown

Using "Test Setup and Test Teardown" prepare the initial state before the tests run and perform the cleanup after the tests are completed.

The Exercise is now to adapt the test script in such a way that the preparatory keywords for opening the website and logging in end up in the "Test Setup" and the closing keywords end up in the "Test Teardown".

To do this exercise you need the following commands:

- Test Setup "*Navigate to home and login*"
- Test Teardown "*Log out and Close Browser*"

Tip: Wait a few seconds to close the browser by using a "sleep" command from the BuiltIn library: https://robotframework.org/robotframework/latest/libraries/BuiltIn.html

Exercise robot-5: Resource files

So far you have included all test data, sections, keywords in your test script.

The task is now to modify the test script in such a way that keywords are placed in a separate resource file.

Bonus Exercise: Try transferring money to another (internal) account.

To do this exercise you need the following commands:
- Resource keywords.resource
- *** Keywords ***

Exercise robot-6: Variables

So far you have hard coded all variables data in your test script.

Exercise: Create a separate section where the variables from the test script are grouped in a separate file.

To do this exercise you need the following commands:
- Resource variables.resource
- *** Variables ***

Example:

```
*** Variables ***
${VARIABLE}            An example string
${ANOTHER VARIABLE}    This is pretty easy!
${INTEGER}             ${42}
@{STRINGS}             one          two            kolme          four
@{NUMBERS}             ${1}         ${INTEGER}     ${3.14}
&{MAPPING}             one=${1}     two=${2}       three=${3}
@{ANIMALS}             cat          dog
&{FINNISH}             cat=kissa    dog=koira
```

Exercise robot-7: Data Driven tests

So far you have based your test script on one user, i.e. John Smith.

Make your test in such a way that you can perform the same test with 2 users.

Create a user via the 'Register' function on the homepage of the site.

To do this exercise you need the following commands:

```
*** Settings ***
Test Template  Login Test

*** Test Cases ***
User John Smith    john  demo
User Jane Doe      jane  demo

*** Keywords ***
    Login Test
```

You already have the content of the “Login Test” in your keywords.resource file, but then you need to add this:

```
Login Test
    [Arguments]  ${username}  ${password}
```

For more information, see:
https://robotframework.org/robotframework/latest/RobotFrameworkUserGuide.html#test-templates

Extra: Exercise robot-RequestLoan: Request Loan

Apply for a loan of $10,000 with a monthly repayment of $100 and check whether the new account exists and that there is an initial deposit.

Use the keywords and the variables files.

Also try to obtain a larger amount and then capture the error message.

Tip: in Dev Tools / Elements you can also find a url after the href. Click Link supports the href attribute and link text as identifiers: element id and name attribute. This time use the url to make a test.

Extra: Exercise robot-Register: Create a new user

In this exercise you will learn to create a new user. First clean the data base by using the Admin Page and click on the CLEAN button. See:

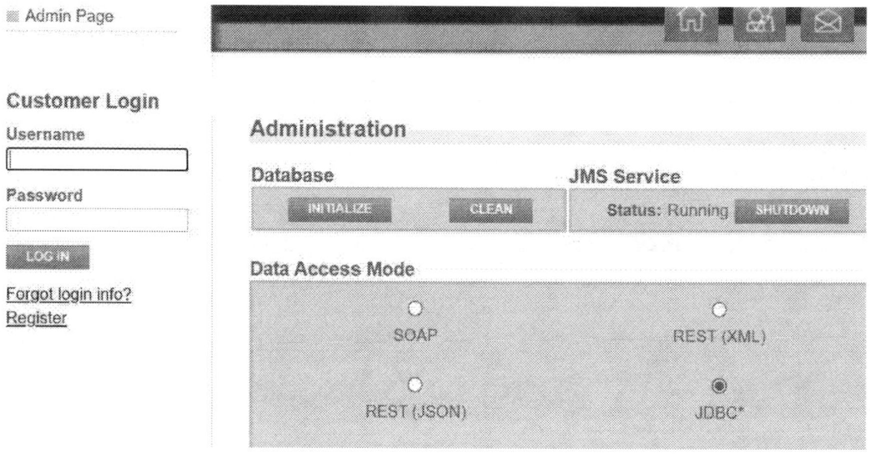

Then follow the Register link.

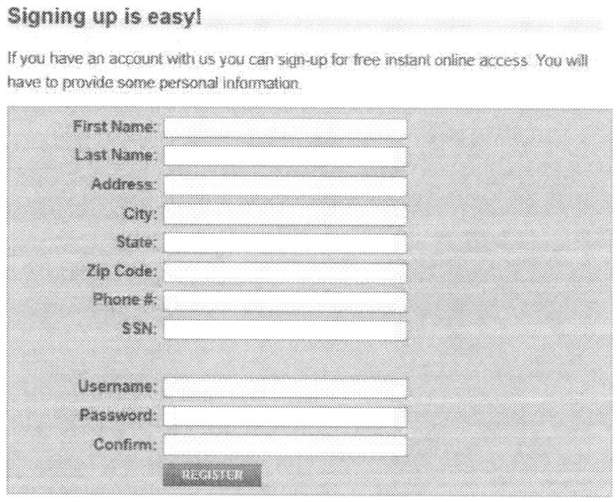

Robot Framework voor API's (webservices)

Exercise robot-8: Accounts Overview via a GET request

The first exercise is a so-called Get request on John Smith's "Accounts overview".
To make sure that the Exercise was successful, you can request the status code '200'.

On the website you can easily find out how the request works.

How to test:

1. Open the ParaBank website via the (chrome) browser and open Dev tools (F12) and click on the 'Network' tab. Log in now with user john and password demo. After logging in, a request called 'accounts' will appear in the 'Network' tab.

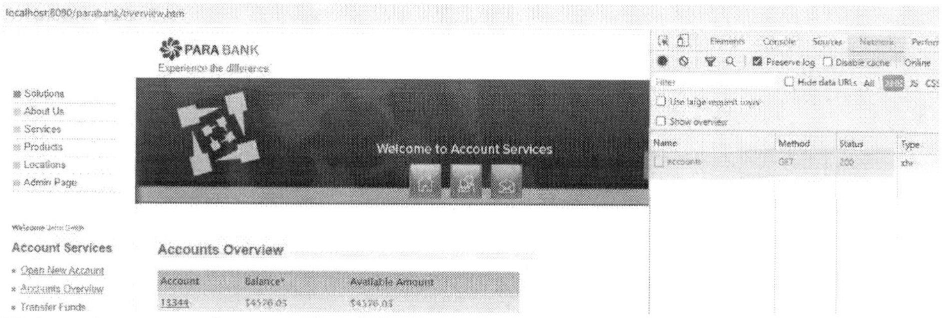

2. Click on the request 'accounts' and the Request URL will be shown as well as the Request Method

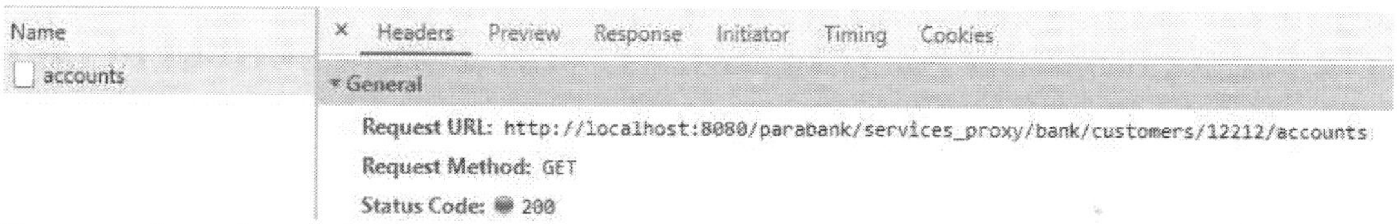

3. Now copy the entire text behind Request URL, i.e. http://localhost:8080/parabank/services_proxy/bank/customers/12212/accounts

In order to continue this exercise, you will also need the RequestsLibrary library and the following keywords in addition to this link:

- Create List https://robotframework.org/robotframework/latest/libraries/BuiltIn.html
- And from: https://marketsquare.github.io/robotframework-requests/doc/RequestsLibrary.html
  - Create Session
  - GET On Session
  - Status Should Be

Tip: use a variable: ${response}= GET On Session parabank ${Accounts}

For further explanation: https://github.com/MarketSquare/robotframework-requests

Exercise robot-9: Open New Account via a POST request

Open New Account and check whether the new account is opened.

To do this exercise you need the following keywords:

- POST On Session
- Status Should Be
- GET On Session

These keywords can also be found in: https://marketsquare.github.io/robotframework-requests/doc/RequestsLibrary.html

Extra exercise: Make a transfer (Transfer Funds) and via a POST request

Transfer money from one account to another account and check whether the transferred money is in the counter account.

To do this exercise you need the following keywords:

- POST On Session
- Status Should Be
- GET On Session

Success? Put your Post on request in a variable and log this variable.

Extra robot-RequestLoanViaAPI: *Apply for a loan (Request Loan) via a POST request*

Apply for a loan of eg $1,000 with a monthly repayment of $100 and check that the new account exists and that there is an initial deposit.

To do this exercise you need the following keywords:

- POST On Session (je wel bekend)
- Log ${response.headers}
- Log ${response.text}
- Log ${response.content}
- Log ${response.json}
- Should Be True (Built-in library)

https://robotframework-thailand.github.io/robotframework-jsonlibrary/JSONLibrary.html

If this is successful, try to request a loan that is refused by borrowing 1 million dollars, for example. What stands out?

To do this exercise you need the following keywords

- POST On Session
- Log ${response.headers}
- Log ${response.text}
- Log ${response.content}
- Log ${response.json}
- Should Not Be True (Built-in library)
- Should Be Equal (Built-in library)

Cypress exercises

https://docs.cypress.io/app/end-to-end-testing/testing-your-app

Exercise cy-1: Visit the website and check if you are on the homepage

https://docs.cypress.io/app/end-to-end-testing/testing-your-app#Step-2-Visit-your-server

To do this exercise you need the following commands:

- cy.visit() https://docs.cypress.io/api/commands/visit.html#Syntax
- cy.title() https://docs.cypress.io/api/commands/title

url: http://localhost:8080/parabank
url: https://parabank.parasoft.com/parabank

In your Cypress project folder C:\CypressTest\cypress\ you have a folder called "e2e". In this folder create a new test file “parabank.cy.js”, if not: copy the code below:

```
describe("My First Test", () => {
  it("Does not do much!", () => {
    expect(true).to.equal(true);
  });
});
```

https://docs.cypress.io/app/end-to-end-testing/writing-your-first-end-to-end-test

Exercise cy-2: Log in with username and password

To do this exercise you need the following commands:

- cy.get() >> https://docs.cypress.io/api/commands/get
- .type() >> https://docs.cypress.io/api/commands/type
- .click() >> https://docs.cypress.io/api/commands/click

Copy the code below:

```
it("should be possible to log in", () => {
//
cy.log('enter your test here);
//
});
```

username: *john*
password: *demo*

Tip: Use F12 (right mouse button: Inspect (CTRL-shift-I) to select elements from the web page. Common term is "Dev Tools".

Exercise cy-3: Open a new account

To do this exercise you need the following commands:

- cy.get()
- cy.click()
- cy.contains()

https://docs.cypress.io/api/commands/contains.html#Syntax

Open a new savings account (SAVINGS) and check whether the new account exists and that there is an initial deposit.

Tip: in Dev Tools / Elements you can also find a link (href) and an id in addition to a class. You can also make a test on these elements.

Extra Exercise cy-4: Cypress.Commands.add

So far you have included all keywords in your test script. In Robot Framework you have already become acquainted with Resource files to build your test script in a modular way.

You can achieve the same thing with Cypress.Commands. Cypress has a standard file: commands.js in the “support” folder.

The Exercise is now to adjust your test script in such a way that as many of the commands (keywords) as possible end up in this file.

To do this exercise you need the following commands:

- In *commands.js*
    - Cypress.Commands.add("login", () => {
      ......
      });
-
    - Cypress.Commands.add("openNewAccount", () => {
      ......
      });
- In *parabank.cy.js*
    - cy.login();
    - cy.openNewAccount();

https://docs.cypress.io/api/cypress-api/custom-commands.html#Syntax

Extra Exercise cy-5: API Test

Cypress provides a great developer experience for testing websites. Normally before we built the UI, we will write various API- and integration tests first with Cypress to ensure the application APIs were working as expected.

Let's look at one of the API tests from the ParaBank app to understand better how to test APIs using Cypress.

In this simple test, we make a **GET** request using cy.request(). We assert that the response returns a **200** status code. See "Exercise robot-8: Accounts Overview via a GET request" if you forgot how to capture the API request from the website.

```
it('Open New Savings Account', () => {
      cy.request({
        method: 'GET',
        url:
'http://localhost:8080/parabank/services_proxy/bank/customers/12212/accounts',
        auth: {
          username: 'john',
          password: 'demo',
        },
      }).then((response) => {
        console.log(response)
        expect(response.status).to.eq(200)
      })
})
```

I think you have enough understanding to come up with the next test on your own.

Open a new SAVINGS account and/or make a transfer (Transfer Funds) and via a POST request.

Transfer money from one account to another account and check whether the transferred money is in the counter account.

And if you want to go all out with Cypress, take a look at: https://www.cypress.io/ and: https://github.com/cypress-io/cypress-realworld-app

[redacted]

GETTING STARTED WITH TEST AUTOMATION

[redacted]

At the time of publication in February 2025, this document reflects the most up-to-date version.

[redacted]

Getting Started with Test Automation

How To Start Automation Testing From Scratch? 8 Steps To Start With.

This software installation guide is made to help you install, uninstall, and upgrade your software and ensuring that you have access to self-help documentation that guide you through setup. If you can't overcome this first hurdle please don't hesitate to send me an email and I will guide you through the setup.

Rob Flier

Email: rob.flier@rftc.nl

Contents

Step 1: Download and Install NodeJS

For most users:

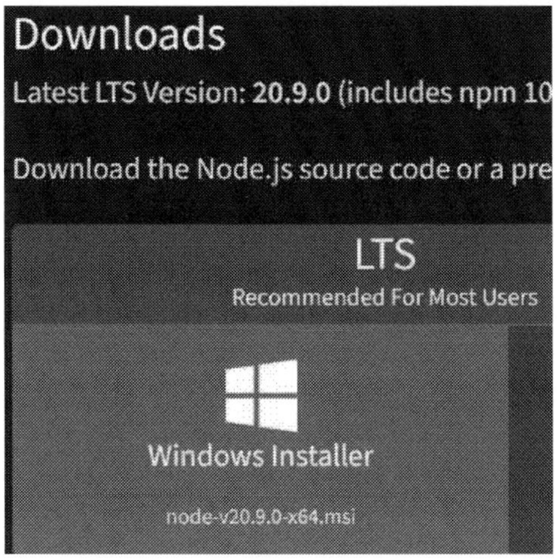

1. Click Next and Accept the terms of the license agreement.

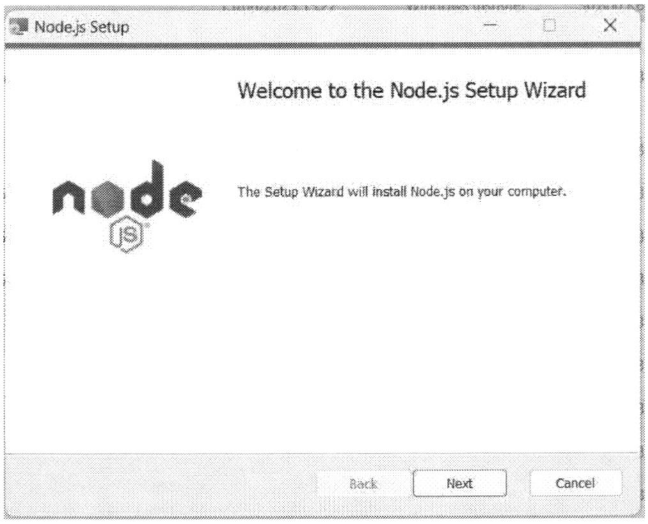

2. Install node.js to: C:\Program Files\nodejs\ by clicking on Next.

3. Click Next until:

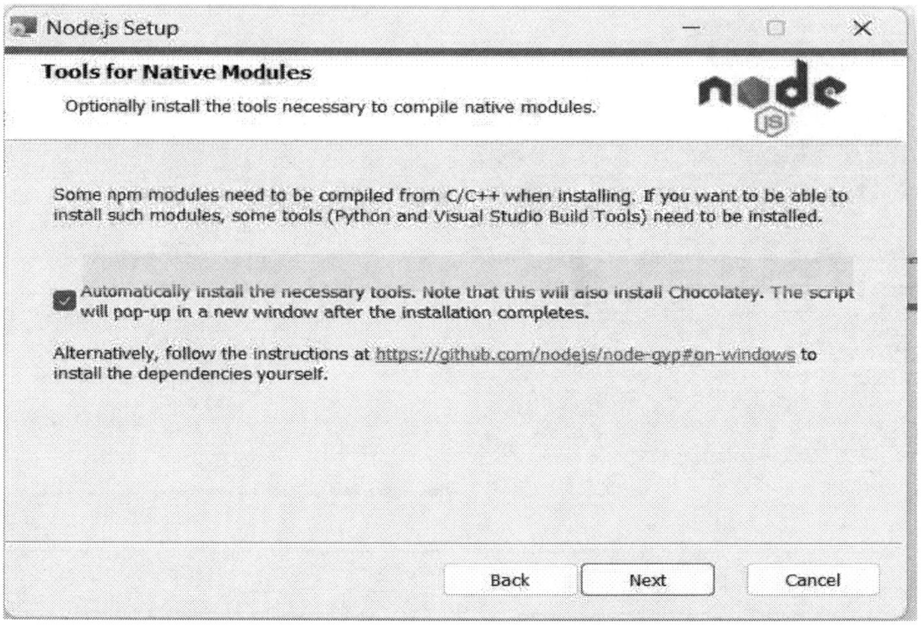

4. Tick the box "Automatically install the necessary tools", click on Next
5. Click on Install

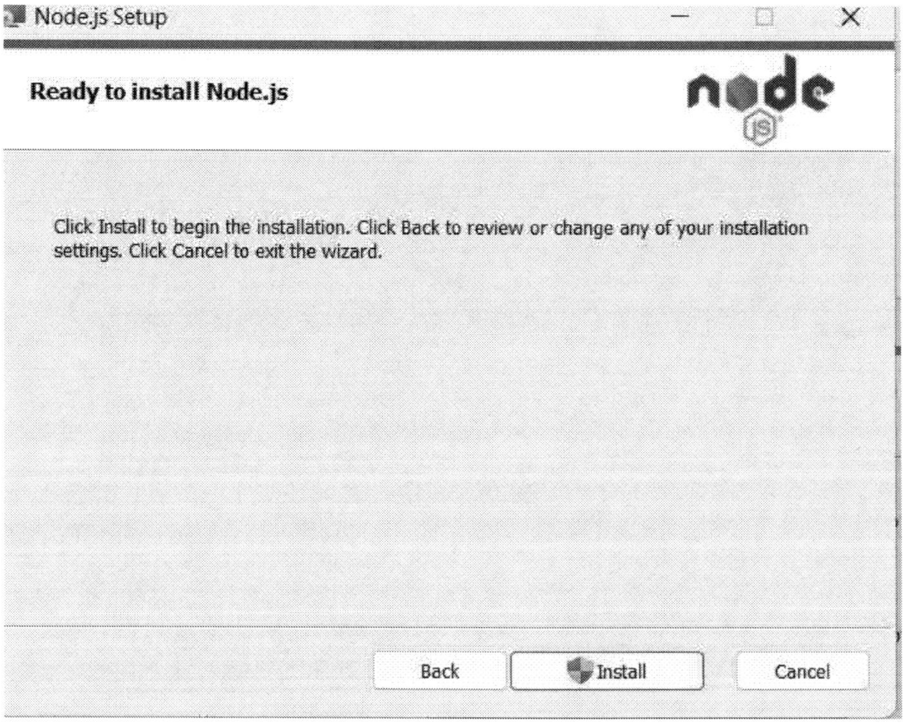

6. Click on Yes to start installation.

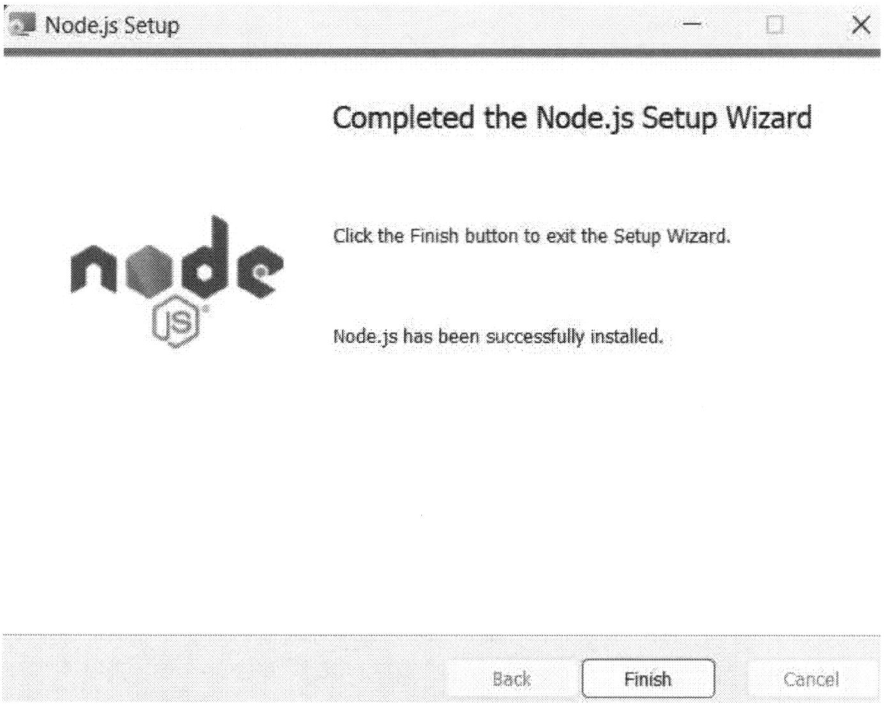

7. Click on Finish

8. This script will install Python and the Visual Studio Build Tools, necessary to compile Node.js native modules. Note that Chocolatey and required Windows updates will also be installed. Press any key to continue .....

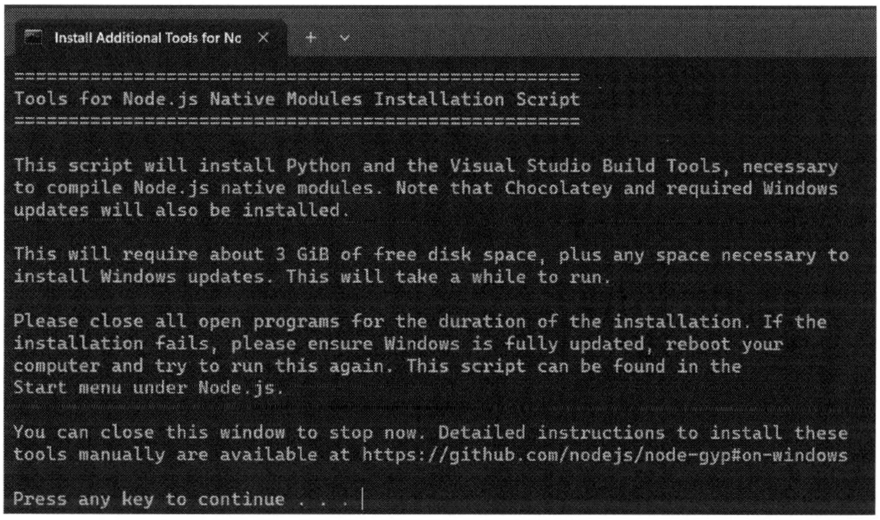

To install these tools manually are available at:
https://github.com/nodejs/node-gyp#on-windows:

npm install -g node-

gyp npm install -g

npm@10.2.3

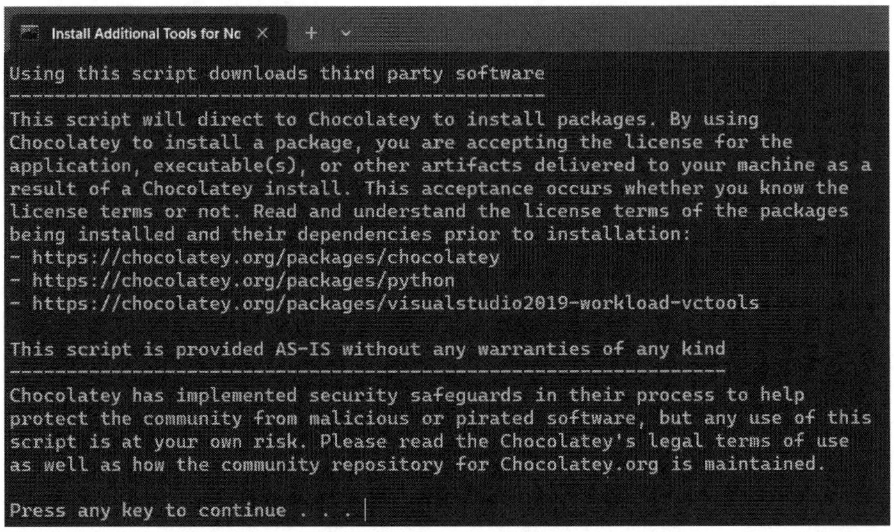

Step 2: Installing Python on Windows

Visit the following website to download Python software.

https://www.python.org/downloads/

Download the latest version for your operating system (eg: Windows)

1. Double-click the Python software to begin the installation.
   The Setup offers an option 'Add Python to PATH. When you check this box, the tool will automatically update the path of Python in environment variables.

2. **Tick both boxes "Use admin privileges" and "Add python.exe to PATH".**

3. Click Install Now

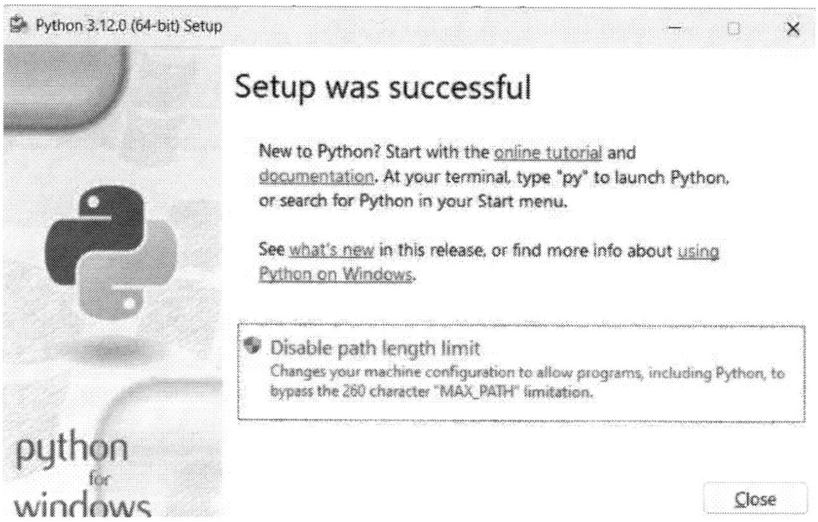

4. Click on Disable path length limit.

   It disables the path length limit by removing the limitation on the MAX_PATH variable. This change will not break anything, or make any negative changes. It will just allow Python to use long path names. It is recommended to disable the path length limit.

5. **Click Close.**
6. **Verify Path settings:**

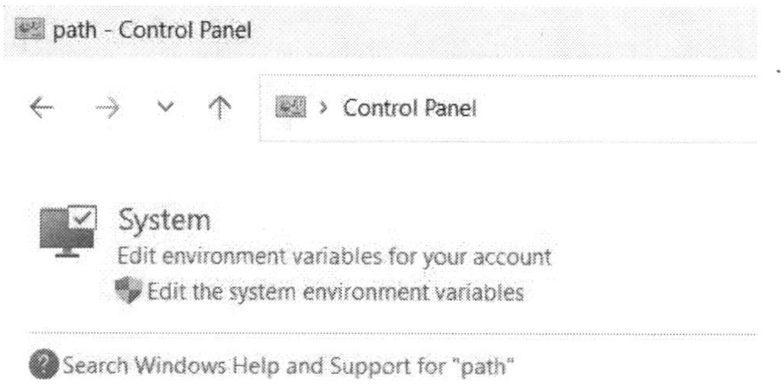

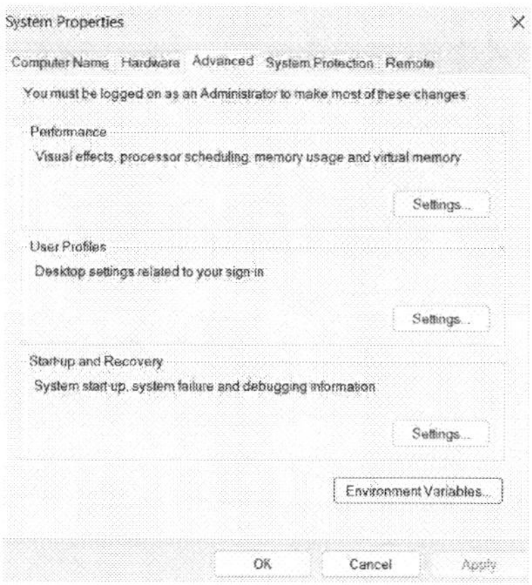

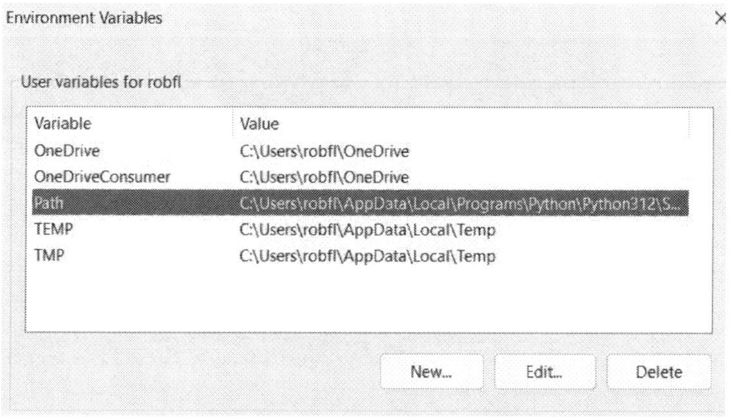

Source: https://projects.raspberrypi.org/en/projects/using-pip-on-windows/4

7. Open a command line tool such as Windows Terminal (the default on Windows 11) or Command Prompt (the default on Windows 10) or Powershell. In the command line, type `python`. If Python is installed, you should see a message like "Python 3. x.x" followed by the Python prompt, which looks like this:

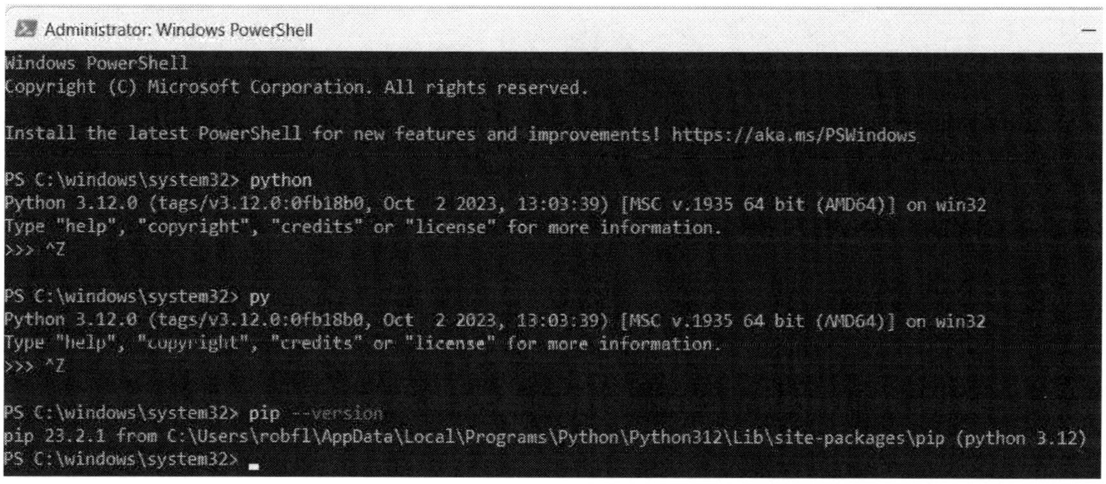

Now, Python and pip are installed and ready for use.

Step 3: Install Robot Framework

1. Open the command prompt and navigate to the python folder and type the following command: pip install robotframework

```
PS C:\RobotFramework> pip install robotframework
Collecting robotframework
  Obtaining dependency information for robotframework from https://files.pythonho
a
  Downloading robotframework-6.1.1-py3-none-any.whl.metadata (7.5 kB)
Downloading robotframework-6.1.1-py3-none-any.whl (699 kB)
   ---------------------------------------- 699.1/699.1 kB 3.7 MB/s eta 0:00:00
Installing collected packages: robotframework
Successfully installed robotframework-6.1.1

[notice] A new release of pip is available: 23.2.1 -> 23.3.1
[notice] To update, run: python.exe -m pip install --upgrade pip
PS C:\RobotFramework>
```

Robot Framework is successfully installed. You can check it using the version command.

robot –version

```
PS C:\RobotFramework> robot --version
Robot Framework 6.1.1 (Python 3.12.0 on win32)
PS C:\RobotFramework>
```

Furthermore we need a few libraries.

2. Install the SeleniumLibrary by typing the following command:
   pip install robotframework-seleniumlibrary

```
Downloading outcome-1.3.0.post0-py2.py3-none-any.whl (10 kB)
Installing collected packages: sortedcontainers, urllib3, sniffio,
ork-seleniumlibrary
Successfully installed attrs-23.1.0 certifi-2023.7.22 cffi-1.16.0
```

3. Install the RequestsLibrary by typing the following command:
   pip install robotframework-requests

```
Installing collected packages: charset-normalizer, requests, robotframework-requests
Successfully installed charset-normalizer-3.3.2 requests-2.31.0 robotframework-requests-0.9.6
PS C:\RobotFramework>
```

4. [Optional] Install Webdrivermanager by typing the following command:
   pip install webdrivermanager

Sources:
https://robotframework.org/robotframework/latest/RobotFrameworkUserGuide.html
https://www.python.org/
https://docs.python.org/3/using/windows.html

Step 4: Download and install Visual Studio Code

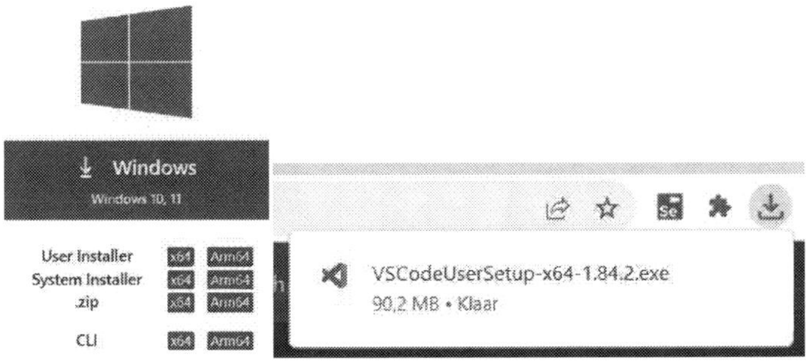

1. Click on downloaded file and accept the agreement, click on Next.
2. Click on Next (leave destination folder as it is).
3. Click on Next. If you like,
    a. create a desktop icon by ticking the box
    b. add "Open with code" by ticking the box(es)
    c. **but in any case keep the box "Add to path" ticked as it is.**

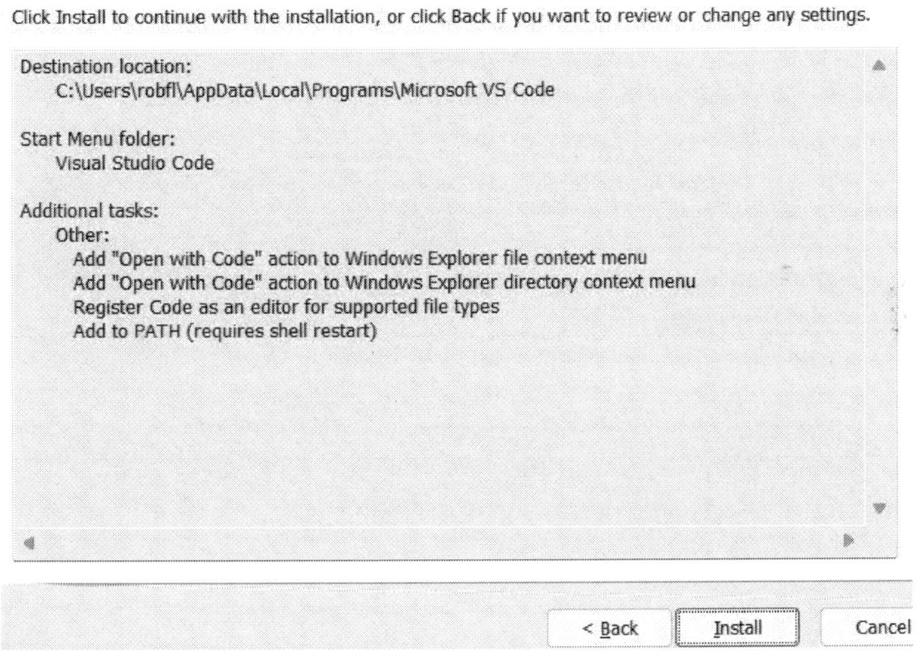

4. Click on Install and on Finish.
5. Create Empty Project Folder in Explorer or CLI

    C:\RobotFramework

    C:\ Cypress
6. Open the folder in Visual Studio Code or Any IDE

    Go to **Visual Studio Code Menu** > Navigate to **File** > Click on **Open Folder** > Choose the newly created Folder from Open Folder Wizard.

7. Install robotframework language server via Extensions (CTRL+Shift+X)

Step 5: Install Cypress

Source: https://www.browserstack.com/guide/how-to-run-cypress-test-automation

Cypress is a NodeJS based automation tool, available as an npm package. Cypress can be also downloaded as an installer, but the recommended way is to install from npm.

1. Create package.json

   The **package.json** helps track all the packages installed for the Cypress automation framework, and it also helps to create shortcut commands to run the tests.

   In order to create the **package.json**, open **Terminal** in Visual Studio Code Menu (C:\Cypress) and type the command: **npm init**

   On entering npm init in the terminal, it asks for a set of questions.

   Answer them or hit: [Enter]-[Enter] until it finishes.

   Finally, it asks – Is this OK? (yes). Then, hit [**Enter**].

   Now the file named **package.json** is automatically created in the root folder of the project.

2. In the root **Project Folder** (C:\Cypress) > **Terminal** > **type: npm install cypress --save-dev**

   source: https://docs.cypress.io/guides/getting-started/installing-cypress

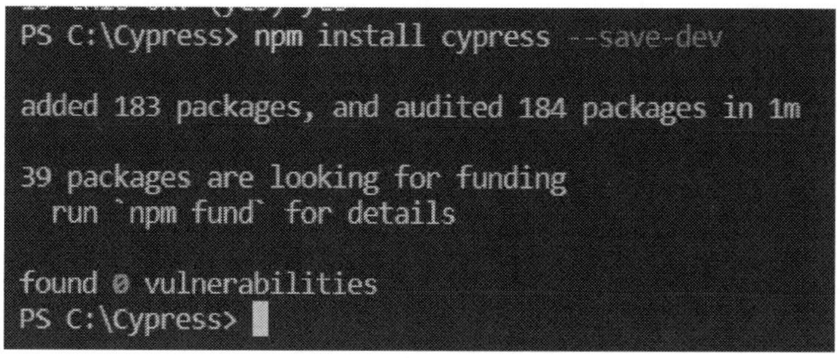

3. Open Cypress Window

Once Cypress packages have been installed, Cypress, by default, configures some folders. Typically 4 folders will be created inside the Cypress folder namely plugins, support, integration, fixtures – the first time when the tester opens Cypress.

In order to open the Cypress window, use one of the following commands: node ./node_modules/cypress/bin/cypress open

Or: **npx cypress open**

See also: https://docs.cypress.io/guides/getting-started/opening-the-app

On entering the above command, execution begins:

Upon successful completion of this command, the Cypress window launches, as seen below:

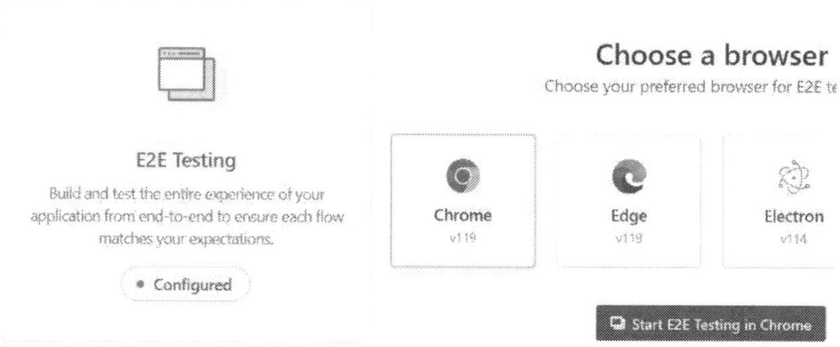

Click on E2E Testing and click on the button: Start E2E Testing in Chrome

If you like, choose scaffold examples.

Click on Specs and click on todo.cy.js

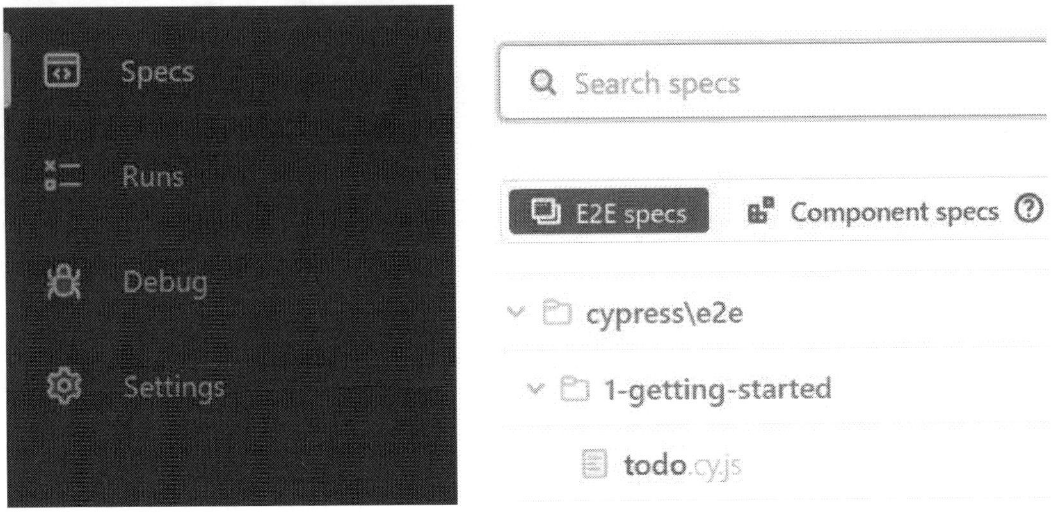

As mentioned earlier, this command also prepares the framework in the background.

It creates a Cypress folder in the project directory, and the Cypress folder will have subfolders like integration, fixtures, plugins, and support.

Now the Project Folder looks like below:

Let's quickly examine these folders, why they are required:

- **e2e:** This is an important folder. All tests should sit inside this folder, because, by default, Cypress assumes that this is the test folder. Testers can create any number of subfolders inside this.
- **fixtures:** This folder helps keep data files such as **example.json,** which can be read directly inside the test scripts.
- **support:** The support folder contains common files (reusable code, global variables, etc.) that need to be accessed globally inside the framework.

Time to get testing! If you chose to start with E2E Testing, go here:
https://docs.cypress.io/guides/end-to-end-testing/writing-your-first-end-to-end-test

Step 6. Install Selenium IDE plug-in

Open your chrome browser by clicking on the 3 dots (Customize and control Google Chrome), More Tools, Extensions.

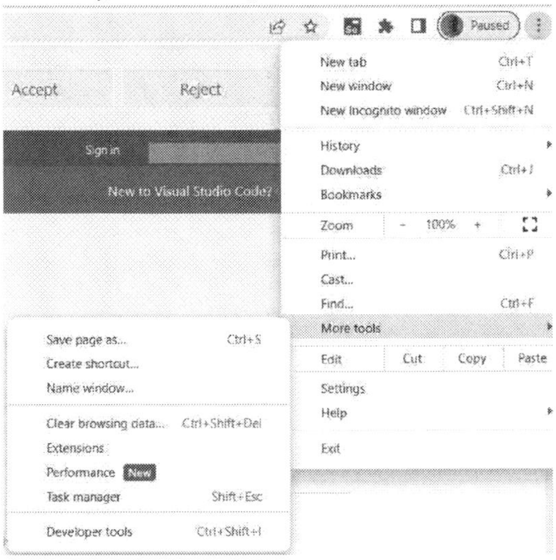

Type in "selenium ide" in search field and the plug-in extension will be revealed. Install the plug-in.

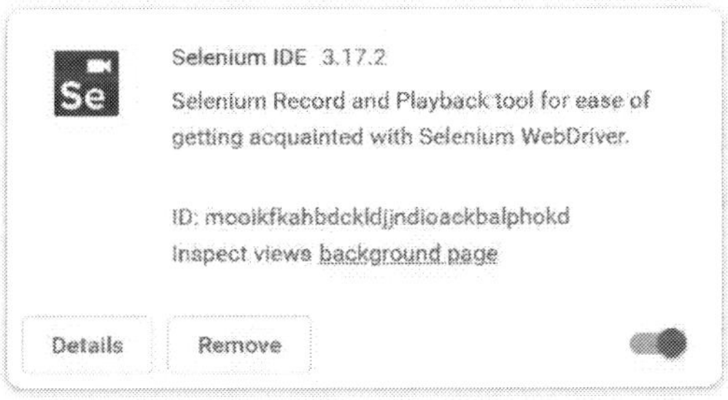

Step 7. Install Postman

Get Postman for Windows: https://www.postman.com/downloads/ and follow the instructions.

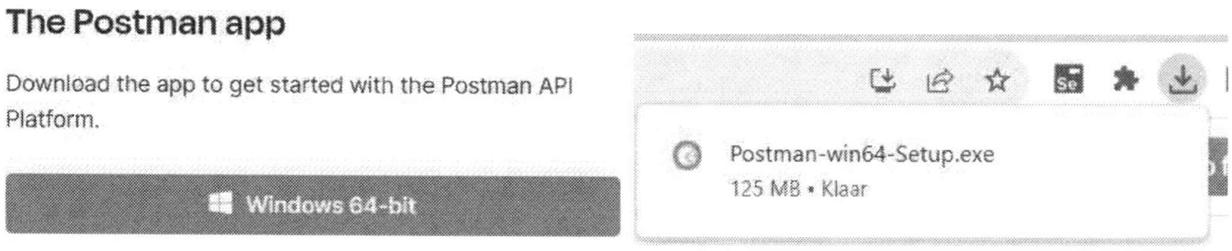

Click on Windows 64-bit and click on downloaded setup file.

Sign up for free or if you don't want to signup you can use the Lightweight API Client instead.

Step 8. Install ParaBank app on localhost

You can run your tests via the public url: https://parabank.parasoft.com/parabank/index.htm but when you want total control of your tests without any disturbance from any other tester / user of the public website you can either install an dedicated version of the website.

Therefore you need to first install a webserver. In my case I installed Tomcat. In below section I will tell you what to do.

Installing Tomcat 9.0

1. JDK (on Windows)
   https://www.oracle.com/java/technologies/downloads/#jdk21-windows

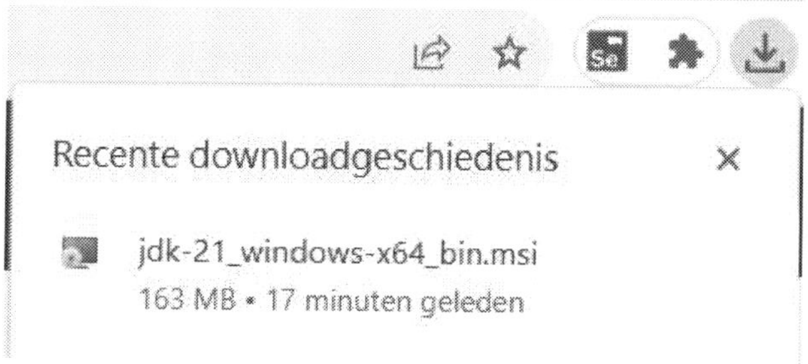

After installation click Next Steps if you want more and if not click Close. Open a Command box or Powershell and type in: java --version

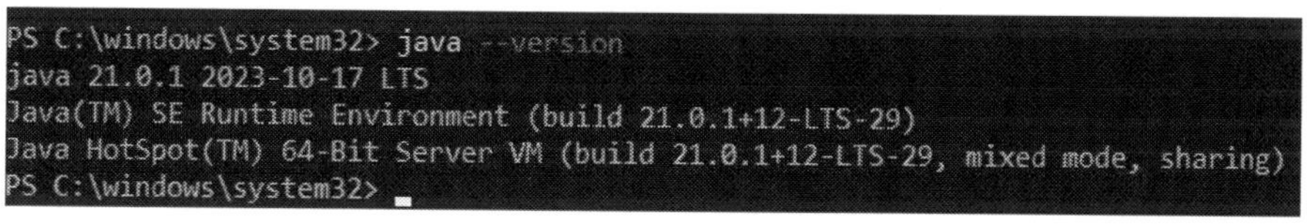

Now you are ready to install Tomcat.

2. Tomcat **9** (https://tomcat.apache.org), pls see also:
   https://www.youtube.com/watch?v=pKMgr8uNvGM

   https://tomcat.apache.org/tomcat-9.0-doc/setup.html#Windows

Note: Do **not** install Tomcat 10. Use of Tomcat 10 onwards should be aware that, as a result of the move from Java EE to Jakarta EE as part of the transfer of Java EE to the Eclipse Foundation, the primary package for all implemented APIs has changed from javax.* to jakarta.*. This will almost certainly require code changes to enable applications to migrate from **Tomcat 9** and earlier to Tomcat 10 and later. **The parabank web application will not work!**

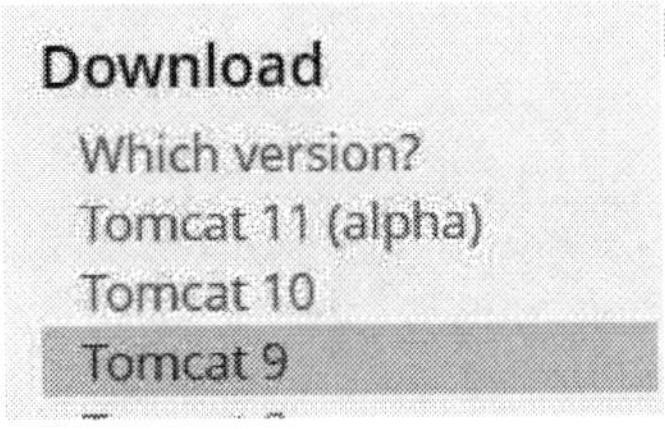

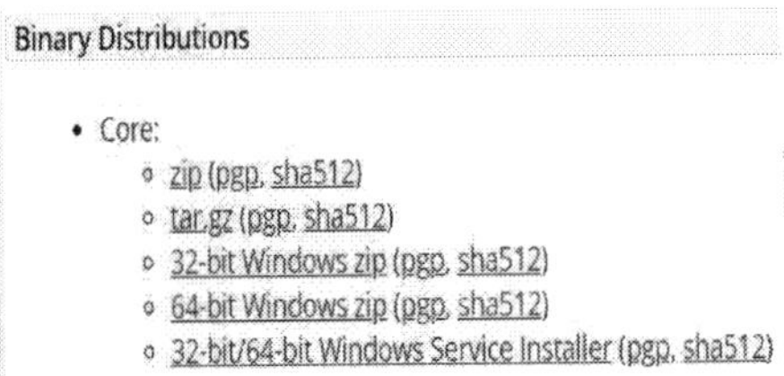

Click on the Installer, Click Next to continue. Click "I Agree", tick all boxes:

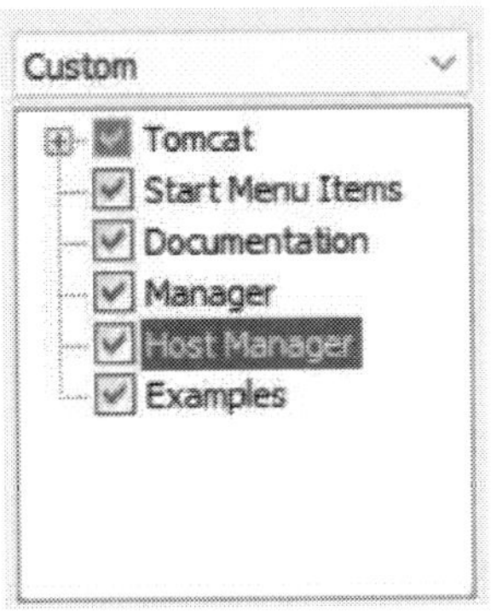

and click Next.

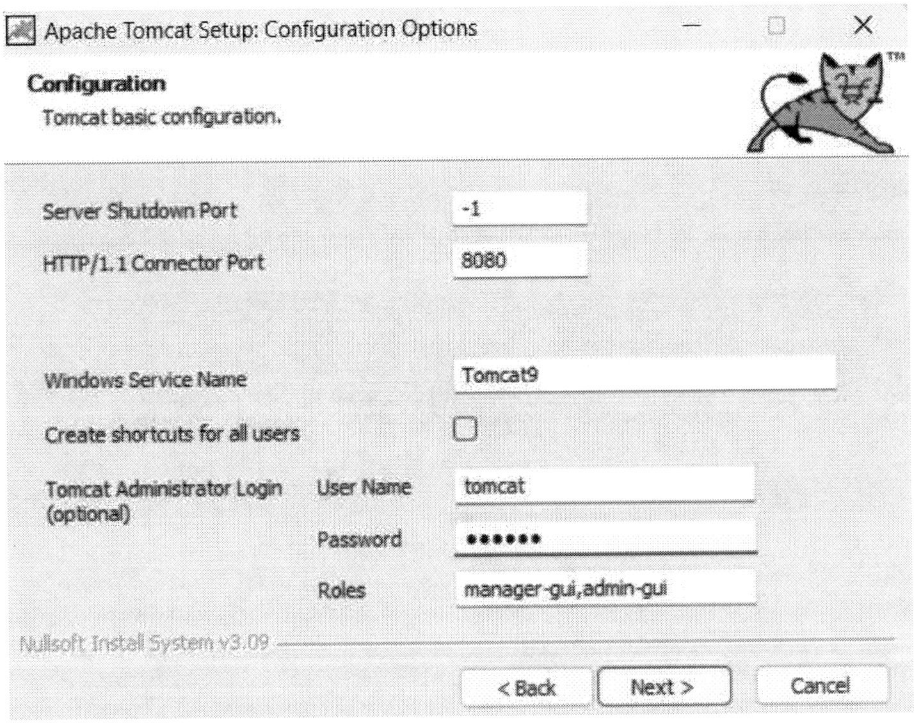

Fill in User Name *tomcat* with password: *s3cret* and click Next.

Verify the path settings:

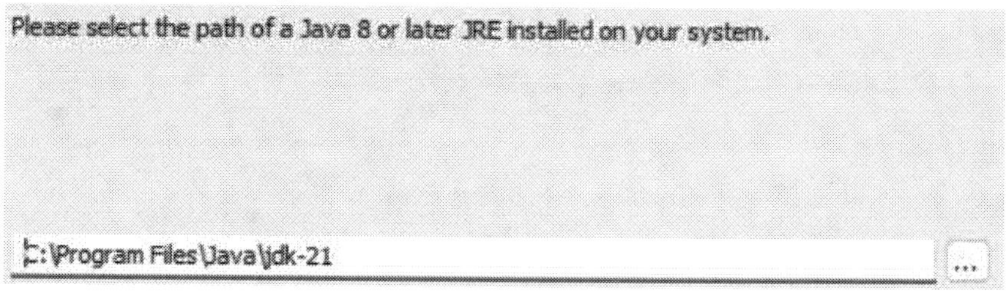

Click Next.

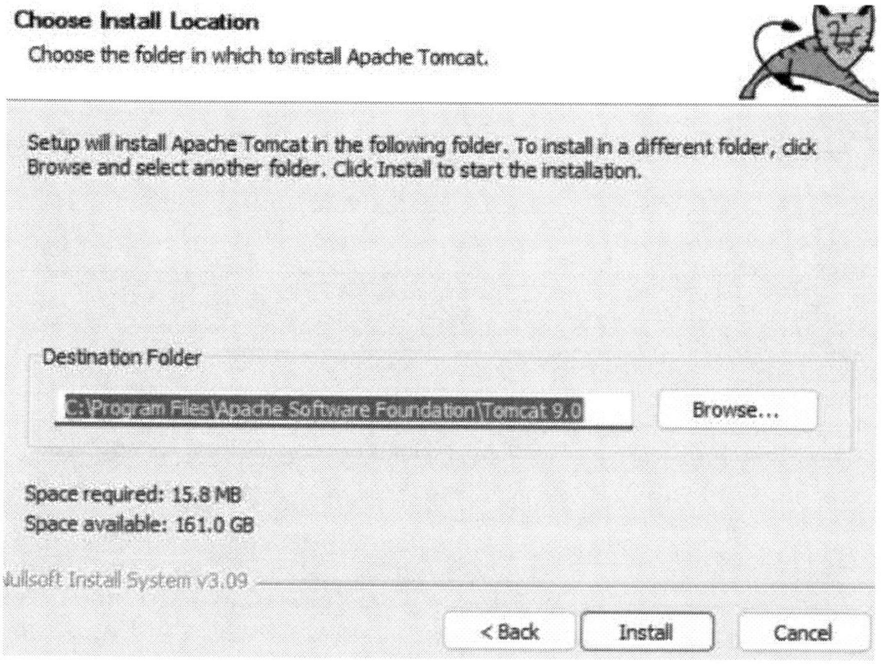

Don't change the destination folder, click on Install.

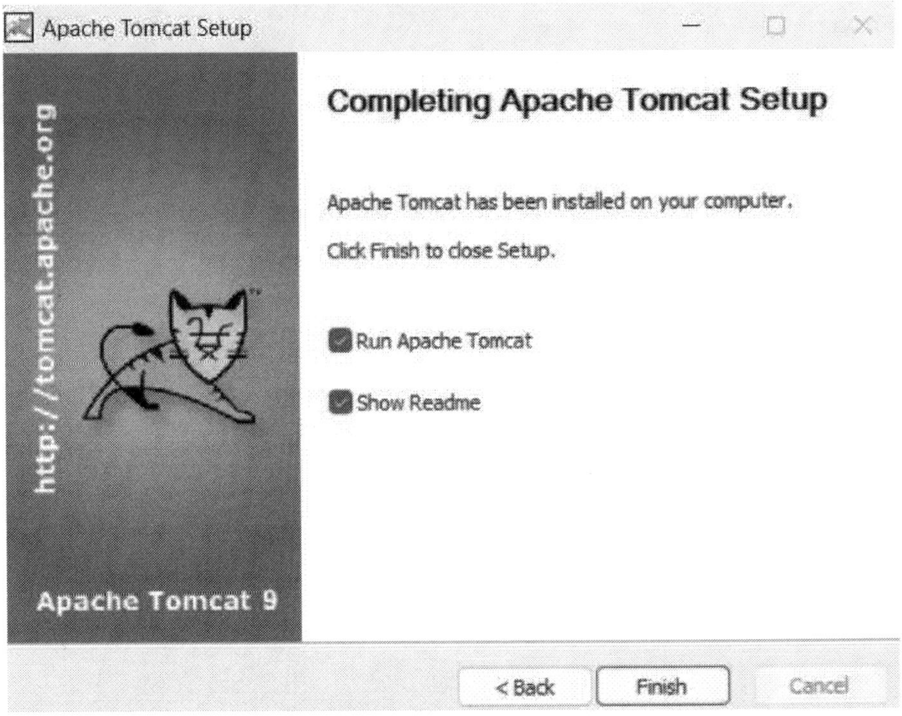

Click on Finish.

After succesful installation open services in Windows menu by typing in: services and a below window is opened. You can see Apache Tomcat is running. You can stop and start the service at will or you can start automatically after reboot.

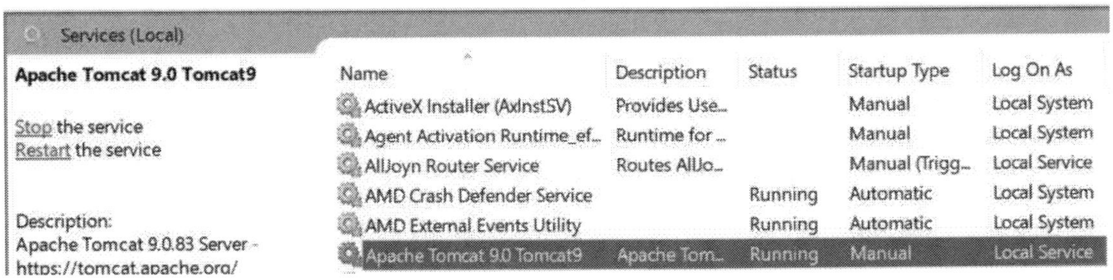

In case you want to start the webserver automatically: right click on the blue line above and open the properties:

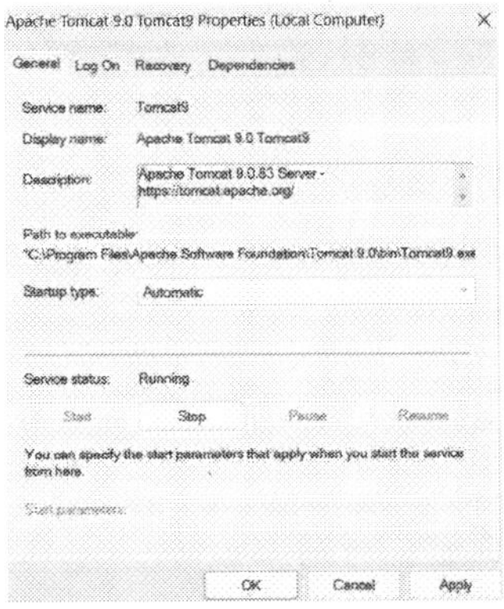

Download and install parabank.war

Pls see *WeTransfer* link or git repository and download the war file:

1. Open Explorer and open: C:\Program Files\Apache Software Foundation\Tomcat 9.0**webapps**
2. Open the folder
3. Unzip (extract) (*) the war file in this directory:

C:\Program Files\Apache Software Foundation\Tomcat 9.0**webapps**

After the extraction the folder is filled with these folders and files:

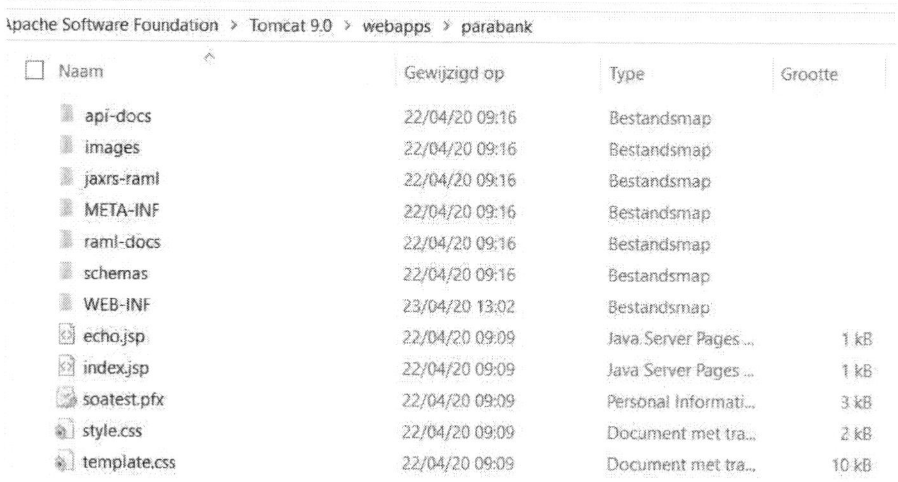

(*) For extraction you can use a tool like WinZip, 7-Zip or WinRar.

Running parabank on localhost

Restart Tomcat webserver via *Services*, via the Windows logo key.

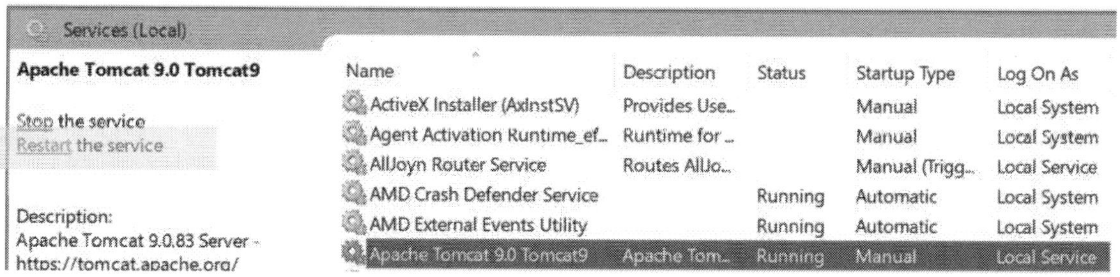

Click on Restart and you will notice that service is stopping and starting.

Open your (chrome) browser and type in: http://localhost:8080/parabank

The website will be presented.

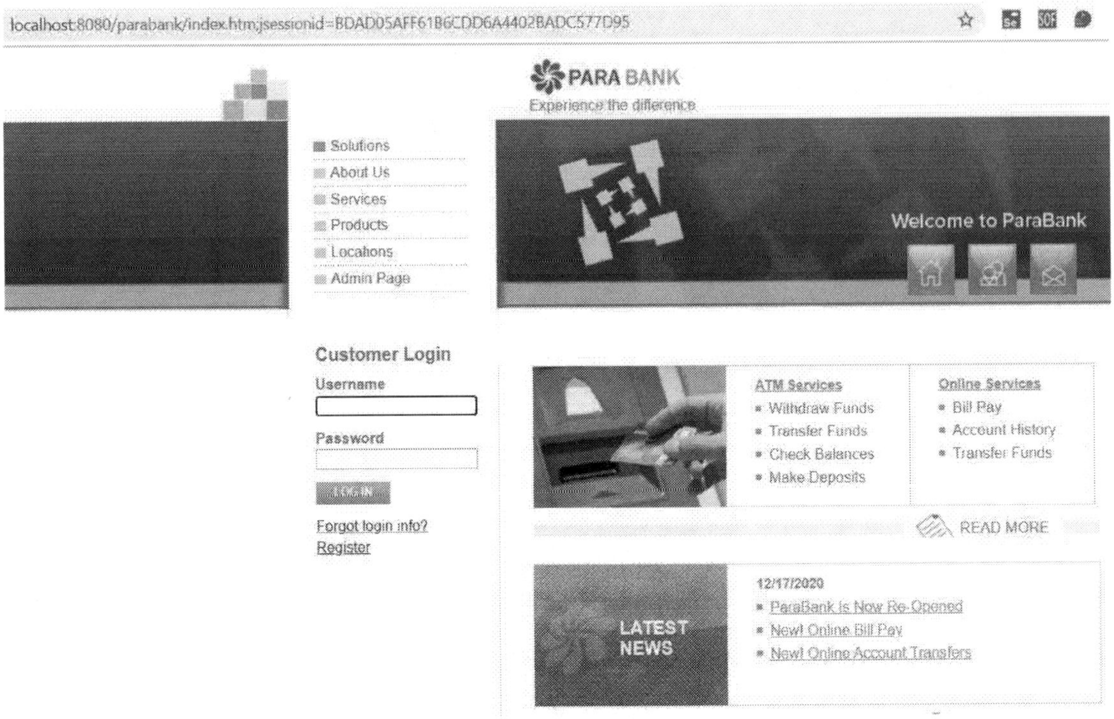

Log in with user: *john* and password: *demo* to verify if all's well.

That will be fine for now.

When everything is finished your installation is successfully executed.

You are now able to use all tools.

Made in the USA
Monee, IL
11 November 2026

68276379R00085